The Fractured Metro

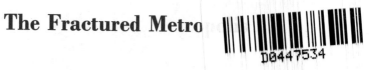

Also by Jonathan Barnett

The Elusive City
Introduction to Urban Design
Urban Design as Public Policy

The Fractured Metropolis

*Improving the New City,
Restoring the Old City,
Reshaping the Region*

Jonathan Barnett

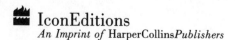
IconEditions
An Imprint of HarperCollins*Publishers*

First paperback edition published 1996.

Designed by Abigail Sturges

The Library of Congress has catalogued the hardcover edition as follows:
Barnett, Jonathan.
    The fractured metropolis : improving the new city, restoring the
    old city, reshaping the region / Jonathan Barnett.—1st ed.
        p. cm.
        "Icon editions."
        Includes index.
        ISBN 0-06-430396-9
        1. City planning—United States.   2. Urban renewal—United States.
    3. Regional planning—United States.   I. Title.
    HT167.B38 1995   94-40811
    307.76'0973—dc20

ISBN 0-06-430222-9 (pbk.)

96 97 98 99 00 CC/RRD 10 9 8 7 6 5 4 3 2 1

Contents

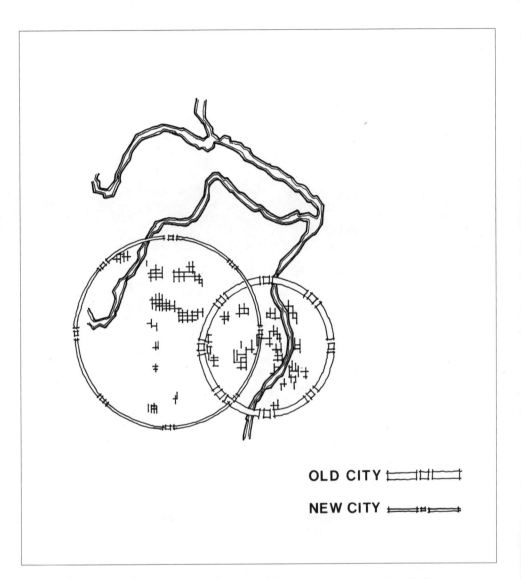

OLD CITY

NEW CITY

1. The urbanized areas of the old city are shown within the first circle, which encloses St. Louis, Missouri, its original suburbs to the west, and East St. Louis and Granite City, Illinois, across the Mississippi River. Downtown St. Louis is on the periphery of the new city, which centers on Clayton and other urbanized former suburbs to the west along the Route 40 and Interstate 70 corridors.

1

Introduction:
The Fractured Metropolis

A merican cities are splitting apart. Traditional downtowns still have their ring of old urban neighborhoods, but nearby suburban villages and rural counties have been transformed into a new kind of city, where residential subdivisions extend for miles and shopping malls and office parks are strung out in long corridors of commercial development.

The old city contains most of the deteriorated housing, the high-crime areas, and what is left of the original smokestack industries, plus the office, government, and cultural concentration downtown, and the fashionable districts of fifty or a hundred years ago, which may still be attractive places to live.

The new city has more than half the recently built office space, many of the best shops, the cleanest industries. Its residential areas are mostly middle or upper income; although lots may be small, houses and apartments are large, luxurious, and new; so are the schools.

The old city is fighting for its life: its tax base is in danger; its schools are in trouble; its streets are unsafe. Although the development boom of the 1980s has subsided, the new city is still prosperous and peaceful, except where its sprawling growth has enveloped older communities with problems of their own.

This division between old cities and new has been created in the last generation. It is different from the familiar separation of rich and poor neighborhoods, or of city and suburb. It affects the new metropolis in the Sun Belt or on the West Coast as much as older urban concentrations in the Northeast and Middle West.

The new city in metropolitan St. Louis centers on Clayton, still a suburb but now also a major office location, and extends to include development along the U.S. 40 and Interstate 70 corridors. A circle encompassing these new urbanized areas takes in the desirable western neighborhoods of the city of St. Louis; but most of the circle includes recently built outlying residential districts that are more connected to new office parks, factories, and shopping malls than to the old city center [1]. A similar new city can be found north of Baltimore, centered on Towson; northwest of Chicago around Schaumberg; or east of Phoenix, around Tempe and Scottsdale. The same kind of diagram could be drawn for Miami/Coral Gables, Dallas/North Dallas, Seattle/Bellevue, Minneapolis/Bloomfield, Houston/Houston Galleria, San Diego/La Jolla, Atlanta/North Atlanta, Pittsburgh/Monroeville. Even a relatively small metropolitan area like Charleston, South Carolina, has split into Charleston/North Charleston, and many a small-town Main Street has been deserted for a new, outlying shopping mall.

Bigger urban regions can have more than one new city. The Philadelphia metropolitan area has one around Valley Forge and King of Prussia, northwest of the old downtown, and a second around Cherry Hill, northeast of Camden, New Jersey. It is possible to make a diagram that shows three new cities in metropolitan Washington, D.C., and four around New York [2].

The separation between old and new city began with the spread of post–World War II residential development, supported by federal mortgage insurance and the mobility conferred by car ownership. This migration to the suburbs made possible the first shopping malls and suburban corporate headquarters. Next, factories moved from constricted urban areas to expansive greenfield locations, a massive relocation process sustained by the new interstate highways, which made railside connections optional. The factories drew people from the old urban neighborhoods, generating demand for more new houses and shops. Then, as more women entered the workforce, the suburban labor market could support more and more offices.

New expressways built to serve old commuting patterns instead drew development outward; the beltways and ring roads designed to help long-distance travelers bypass cities became a new variety of

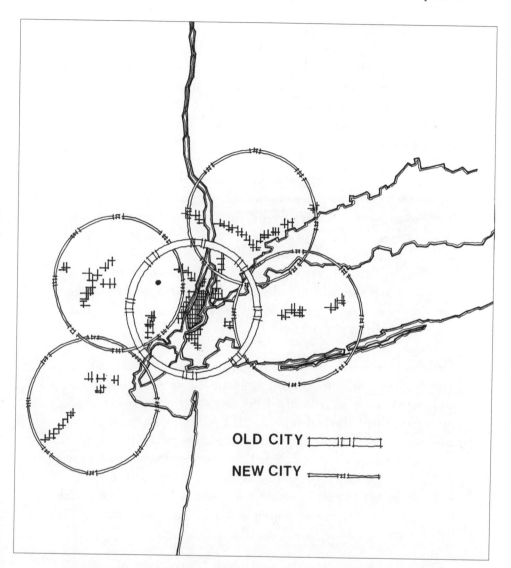

2. The old New York City metropolitan area is surrounded by four new cities.
One includes suburban areas north and east of Manhattan, with major
urbanization along the Cross Westchester Expressway, and in downtown White
Plains, New York, and downtown Stamford, Connecticut, which used to be small
suburban business districts. A second new city is located around Morristown, New
Jersey, with the urbanized area extending northward to Whippany, Parsippany,
and Troy Hills and south to formerly rural communities like Bernardsville and
Basking Ridge. A third new city extends along the Route 1 corridor on both sides
of Princeton, New Jersey, while Long Island has its own new city, with the main
focus around Huntington. The Manhattan business center is peripheral to the
area of influence of each of these new urban concentrations. The urbanized New
Jersey shore might be considered a fifth new city.

main street. By the mid-1970s, shopping centers could be found around the whole periphery of the city, and the majority of office space was being built away from downtowns in office parks or highway commercial strips, conveniently near the homes of top executives or by the airport. Back in the old city, downtown stores began to close, factories were abandoned, and whole neighborhoods became derelict.

The pace of change accelerated in the 1980s. Builders constructed master-planned communities of thousands of new houses, and other rural areas were transformed by the combined effect of many smaller developments. Much of this new housing was built at densities that used only to be found in close-in urban neighborhoods: large houses on small lots, attached townhouses, and garden apartments. In the meantime, malls and office parks converged into corridors and concentrations equivalent in importance to traditional city centers.

The older cities worked hard to fight the trends and keep the tax base necessary to support aging residential neighborhoods, the accumulated stock of subsidized housing, and ever-growing social programs. Cities devised sophisticated public-private partnerships and transformed the design of downtown: assembling land, building parking garages; manipulating the tax code for office buildings and hotels; constructing cultural centers, convention centers, and festival market places; promoting downtown housing; improving the streetscape. Cities also used subsidies to retain industry in urban locations, or to lure it back.

These efforts have often worked. The rapid expansion of urban areas in the 1980s was accompanied by a downtown development boom. But the shiny new skyline and elegant downtown mall draw attention away from devastated inner-city neighborhoods, and from schools and social services struggling to keep up with accelerating numbers of people in need. Even the cities like Portland, Oregon, Minneapolis, and Boston that have been the most successful in renewing themselves look to the future with uneasiness, as do big centers that once thought they were invulnerable, like New York, Chicago, and San Francisco. Other cities, such as Camden, New Jersey, or Gary, Indiana, have such severe problems that it seems impossible for them to solve them on their own. In the older parts of every city, factories continue to leave and offices and stores to close; in some neighborhoods abandonment and deterioration have been followed by situations where law and order seem to be breaking down completely.

Meanwhile the developing new city has its own problems. For years, the most rapidly growing suburban towns and counties continued to assume they were satellites of established city centers. They were not prepared to become centers themselves. Their zoning and subdivision ordinances had been written when a major change meant adding a few dozen houses, or building a new supermarket on Main Street. Planning boards struggled with development proposals for huge shopping centers, massive office parks, residential subdivisions of hundreds and even thousands of acres. There were no precedents for the scale of these new developments or the speed with which they were constructed. Because each component was proposed separately, by competing developers, the shape of the new city did not emerge until it was accomplished fact. It became far more fragmented, ugly, and inefficient than if it had been planned in advance by either government or a single entrepreneur.

The most obvious defects of the new city are traffic gridlock, the deteriorating natural environment, bad planning and shoddy construction. Many strip shopping centers and jerry-built town-house and garden-apartment clusters have a doubtful economic future. There are also more subtle problems of personal alienation and social disconnection.

Older cities and suburbs grew up around rail transportation systems, which concentrated development within walking distance of train stations and transit stops, or in corridors close to trolley routes. Out in the newly developing areas everyone at first assumed that automobile access on local roads and highways would be sufficient, and part of the attraction of moving a business to the new city was freedom from traffic congestion and the old commute downtown.

Today many newly urbanized areas experience almost continuous rush-hour conditions, with short breaks in the midmorning and midafternoon. Saturday, when everyone is out doing errands, can be the worst day of all. Fewer people commute along the highways from suburb to downtown and more commute from place to place within the new city, often on roads that were never planned for heavy traffic, and have been widened and improved ad hoc. Attempts to encourage minivan routes or car pools have relatively little success; and the new city is too spread out and fragmented to be served effectively by the minimal bus systems found in most areas.

Each shop or office building has to provide its own parking, so each structure is surrounded by asphalt, fragmenting development even more. Individual companies or investors seeking relief from traffic and from squalid corridors of continuous parking lots, garish signs, and disorganized, contending architecture seek new sites on the urban fringe. Others soon follow and the pattern repeats itself, accompanied by even more scattered development and traffic.

One of the reasons for escaping the old city was to enjoy the natural environment, an ambition often frustrated by rapid urbanization. Losing familiar scenery to standardized houses, massive buildings, and parking lots strikes many people as sufficient reason to change development policies, but the issues go beyond aesthetic preferences. Regrading hillsides, which requires removing natural vegetation, placing streams in culverts, or paving over large areas for parking were all acceptable techniques for managing development when they were exceptions within a largely natural environment. Once whole regions are regraded, paved, and channeled, there is a high risk of undesirable environmental change: flooding, soil erosion, greater temperature extremes, falling water tables, contaminated aquifers.

The expanding city also requires more and more natural resources to sustain it—not just land, but the fuel for all the extra automobile trips, water supplies for newly urbanized areas, and the construction materials to duplicate the buildings and infrastructure left behind in the old city. As natural systems become overloaded in the new city, air and water pollution, somewhat improved in the old city after years of expensive upgrading of factories and infrastructure, become serious problems over an increasingly large area.

There is also an uneasy feeling that life in the new city has an alienated quality. Out in two-acre-zoning country, old ideas of neighborhood and neighborliness are hard to sustain: borrowing a cup of sugar from the house next door might mean a five-minute walk. People living in new town-houses or garden apartments are close to their neighbors, but without street-life and local schools or services they have all the disadvantages of concentrated urban life without the amenities. The parent as chauffeur has become a familiar description; when most houses are built on large lots or in isolated clusters, schools and parks are inevitably out of walking distance for all but a few children, and school friends can live long distances apart. Domestic errands also take a lot of driving time when residential zoning districts can extend for miles, without permitting so much as a convenience store. Shops and services are zoned into narrow strips of land along a few main highways, meaning that customers must drive from store to store, generating more trips and more congestion. For some, spending a lot of time in a car alone may be a welcome respite from frantic offices and demanding home life. Car phones, radios, and tape decks are compensations for solitude; but hours of daily automobile travel have become a necessity for many people whether they like it or not.

Of course, life in the new city is attractive; offering spacious residential neighborhoods with beautifully tended lawns and gardens, gatehouse protection, offices in parklike settings, all kinds of convenient shopping—hence the new city's continuing ability to draw the vitality out of older areas. Most people who have moved to the new city are aware that they have adopted a way of life created as an escape from community social responsibilities. At the back of consciousness, they know that the new city cannot be a permanent refuge if the old city does not survive and prosper. The split between the old city and the new is irreversible, but the current situation is just a phase in a still evolving pattern. The question is: What will happen next?

Corporate headquarters and research installations are beginning to move to rural sites beyond the new city. Land is easier to find, development approvals are faster, and the journey to work from the new city out to a rural area avoids most of the places where traffic gridlock takes place now. For example, Sears has moved its merchandise division from its tower in downtown Chicago to an office campus in Hoffman Estates, 37 miles from the Loop, and 12 miles farther out than the office concentration in Schaumberg. J. C. Penney has moved to Plano, beyond the northern fringe of the Dallas metropolitan area; Chrysler's new technology center is in Auburn Hills, about 35 miles north of downtown Detroit. Hoffman Estates is way beyond the rapid-transit system and rail network that serves the older parts of metropolitan Chicago; Plano is a long way from south Dallas; Auburn Hills is a long way from Detroit. The corporate decision-makers who chose these locations had to know that very few people from old city neighborhoods would be able to make the commute. If employment centers continue to move out in this way, the new city will be effectively severed from the old.

Corporate offices have been leaving the old city for a long time. Banks, brokerage houses, insurance companies, and public utilities—plus the lawyers and accountants that serve them—have remained in downtown office centers because they need big clerical staffs and thus a central location in the largest possible labor market.

Long-predicted innovations in technology and communication have recently begun to transform these businesses. Back-office clerical activities are moving out of the downtown headquarters building. The first moves were to cheaper space in the same city, but once the back office is at the other end of a telephone wire, or fiber-optic cable, it doesn't seem to matter where it is. Boston's State Street Bank has its back-office operations in suburban Quincy; much of Citibank New York's back office is now in Sioux Falls, South Dakota. Once the front office no longer needs to be next to a big back office, the old city downtown is no longer the only practical headquarters location for financial businesses and utilities.

When United States manufacturing industries lose business to foreign companies and are left with overcapacity in the United States, the logical plants to close are the oldest, in the most constricted urban locations. Most current plant closings are taking place in old factory towns and the older parts of metropolitan areas.

These are disturbing trends. If corporations are choosing rural locations beyond commuting distance for inner-city workers, and if employers no longer need their central-city clerical offices and factories, where does today's old-city resident find tomorrow's job?

People in areas without jobs are going to move if they can: populations are falling in many older cities, while the percentages of people on welfare are rising. As a city's social problems increase and its tax base goes down, it enters a familiar downward spiral of deteriorating maintenance, services, and public safety. The big downtown corporations subscribe to redevelopment plans and send executives to conferences on the future of the city, but if old cities continue to deteriorate, it is only a matter of time before the remaining major businesses start looking seriously for alternatives.

Is the old city a write-off? Is it destined to be replaced by new suburban and exurban development? Only an extraordinarily rich country could even contemplate such a possibility, and it still seems improbable. The replacement cost of buildings, roads, and utility services in any city would be higher than its total assessed valuation plus its entire capital debt; the cost of reproducing the whole urban establishment is probably beyond our national means. Real estate goes through cycles: one investor's disaster is eventually another's opportunity. Business also goes through cycles; Sioux Falls loses jobs in meat packing and gains them in data processing and telemarketing.

But it will take a long time for the business cycle to start solving the problems of cities. The next few decades, all the future that most people can cope with, could easily be a time of dangerous social conflict. The vitality could continue to be drawn from many older cities, making them more and more the places with the most problems and the least resources. Newly developing areas could continue to suffer from a surfeit of growth, creating more and more gridlock, which will require expensive corrective measures, and more degradation of the natural environment, which probably can never be repaired. Experience with the consequences of rapid urbanization leads to more bruising zoning battles, pushing development even farther away from the older urban centers and intensifying the split between old city and new.

In addition to the ethical questions raised by letting people with less and less access to jobs become concentrated into ever more dangerous and deteriorating urban neighborhoods, is such a de facto social policy in anyone's self-interest? Nineteen-sixties radicals used to threaten that unless social and economic injustices were corrected, the cities would burn. The response of the 1970s and 1980s has been for many people to withdraw out of reach of the fire. But is the new city really so invulnerable? And if it can be made so, is this the society we really want?

Restoring the old city means new investments. "You can't solve urban problems by throwing money at them" is the refrain that often greets proposals to spend money on the old city. But investment today in the old city can pay for itself in new jobs, increased property values, and money saved by not building additional roads and utilities on the fringes of the metropolitan area. Because of population declines in the last generation, most old cities have the capacity to accommodate much of the growth anticipated for the entire metropolitan area, potentially an enormous real estate opportunity. The departure of smokestack industries has removed many of the causes of pollution and blight. The immensely valuable network of streets and utilities; the stock of usable older buildings; the existing schools, churches, and parks; the downtown business centers, universities, hospitals, cultural institutions, and attractive urban neighborhoods are all major assets. New money is needed to rebuild public housing projects that had been designed as holding areas and not communities; to restore deteriorating public buildings; to correct the blighting effect of highways, railways, and power lines; and to reclaim derelict industrial areas. Restoring the old city also depends in part on new initiatives to end welfare dependency, improve community policing, and make urban school systems more effective.

It has been a long while since the United States had a normal peacetime economy where investment in city development was routine, as it is today in Europe, Canada, Australia, and Japan. We are still living on the capital put into cities before World War II. New urban investment now is critical, both to reduce development pressures on the new city and to restore older areas, two parts of the same policy. You can't have one without the other.

Growth in the new city has usually been shaped by highway construction and whatever development regulations were already in place: a complex maze of zoning, subdivision, sewer permits, and environmental controls. Developers complain about too many new regulations, but the biggest design and economic problems are caused by the most basic zoning and subdivision provisions, invented generations ago and long outmoded.

Where growth in the new city has been managed successfully, it has required a mix of environmental conservation, new transportation systems, and revised development regulations that create desirable communities compact enough to be served by public transit.

A major investment priority for both the new and old city is a road and transit system that will reintegrate them, at first emphasizing bus service, but also rail links where they are appropriate. The design of this transportation system should be based in part on regional ecology, so that the places most suitable for new development have ready access to transportation, and places that should be protected for environmental reasons are shielded from development pressures. Deployment of such systems will be expensive, but the money that could be used to reintegrate metropolitan regions could easily be wasted on futile local attempts to tie together and support an increasingly spread-out and inefficient new city.

The tradition of home rule leaves planning and development issues to local governments, but metropolitan regions have grown so large that the state has a necessary role as the coordinator for local decisions; and federal aid to states and localities needs to be conditioned on sound regional development policies.

While the U.S. Constitution does not permit the kind of central direction of urban and environmental policy to be found in France, for example, nor will cities, towns and counties let the states assert the kinds of central control wielded by a Canadian province, federal and state governments can still provide revenue sharing to overcome inequalities created when local political boundaries no longer correspond to economic realities. Federal and state governments should also continue to set environmental standards and other kinds of regulations where uniformity from community to commu-

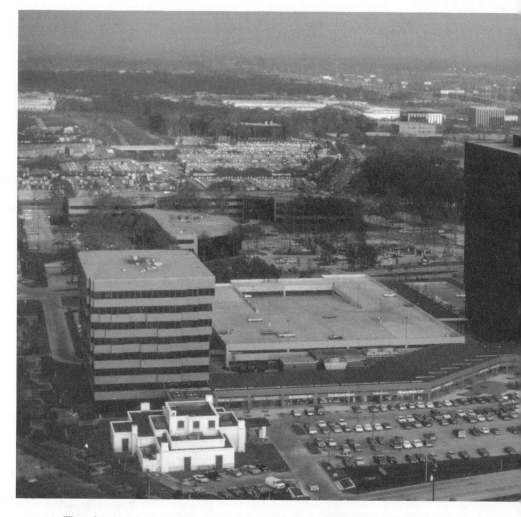

3. This photograph of development in the new city near Houston International Airport shows how downtown activities have escaped from the old urban centers.

nity is essential. Negotiated compacts between states are needed when metropolitan districts cross state boundaries, and federal assistance would help states to support new regional economic and regulatory policies.

Public officials, business executives, developers, planners, designers, environmentalists, social activists, and community leaders have been struggling for decades to keep old cities robust and new cities attractive. It is through their efforts that the quality of new development and the split between old city and new have not become even

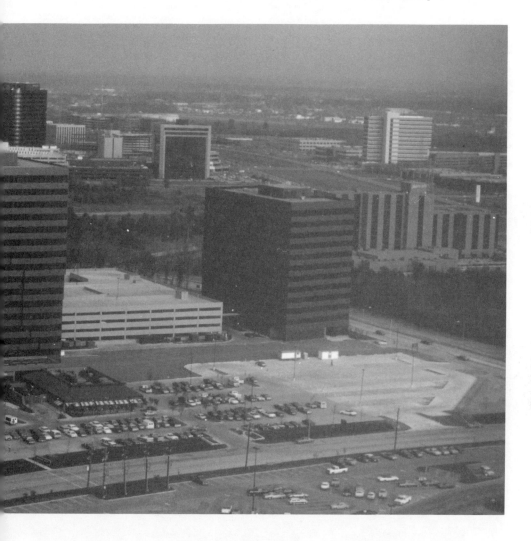

worse. Many battles have been lost, but successful examples already exist of well-planned growth in new locations and of major restorations in old cities. Progress is being made in regional economic and transportation links. This cumulative experience has demonstrated that current trends don't have to define national destiny.

Though it is easy to assume that nothing can be done, this book documents the many promising developments occurring in separate places. Local successes can be turned into policies that will help improve conditions everywhere.

Part I
Improving the New City

2

Accidental Cities or
New Urban Centers

What do you call a place with several big office buildings, two or three department stores, dozens of shops, a first-class hotel, movie theaters, a variety of restaurants, and no sidewalks? Can you say these elements make up a city when the ingredients are spread out over several miles, and most of the land is covered with parking lots? "Edge cities," "urban villages," "technoburbs," or just plain urban sprawl: none of these phrases quite conveys what is happening. Joel Garreau's *Edge City: Life on the New Frontier* is a great description of the phenomenon, but he refrains from evaluating the strangely fragmented way in which development occurs. These new places seem almost accidental, despite the high-powered developers, designers, and public officials who guide the building process.

Three drawings prepared for the Regional Plan Association of New York explain how such places grow up, and show what might have been built instead [4, 5, 6]. In the first sequence, the land around a newly completed highway interchange was zoned for commercial development, a move intended to accommodate gas stations, fast-food restaurants, and other businesses that serve travelers. Instead, the ingredients of a small city center gradually appeared: a hotel, a shopping mall, offices, and industry. Each required some modification of the zoning and a separate approval process, but no one understood what was happening until it was too late.

Lewis Mumford called the highway cloverleaf America's national flower, but even Mumford at his most pessimistic and sarcastic did not imagine broad bands of highway pavement or grasslands owned by the state transportation department permanently enshrined as the centerpiece for so much new development. Someone with business at a suburban office park who stays overnight at a hotel in one quadrant of the cloverleaf will face an intricate drive in the morning to reach the office park diagonally across the intersection. At lunch

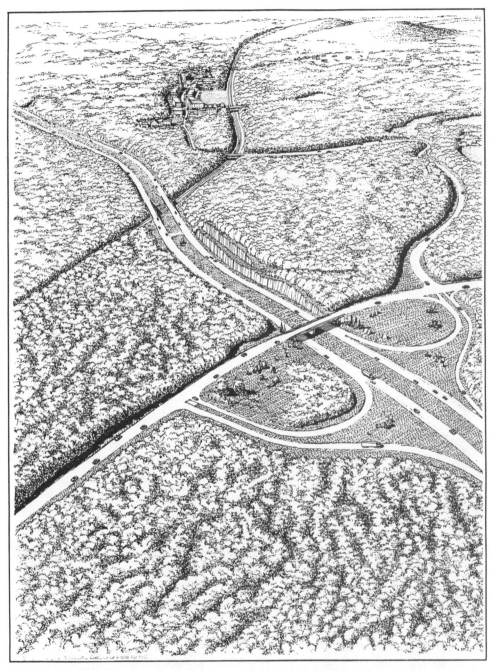

4. *A sequence of drawings prepared for New York's Regional Plan Association showing, first, a typical intersection of highway and secondary road in a suburban location, just after it has been completed.*

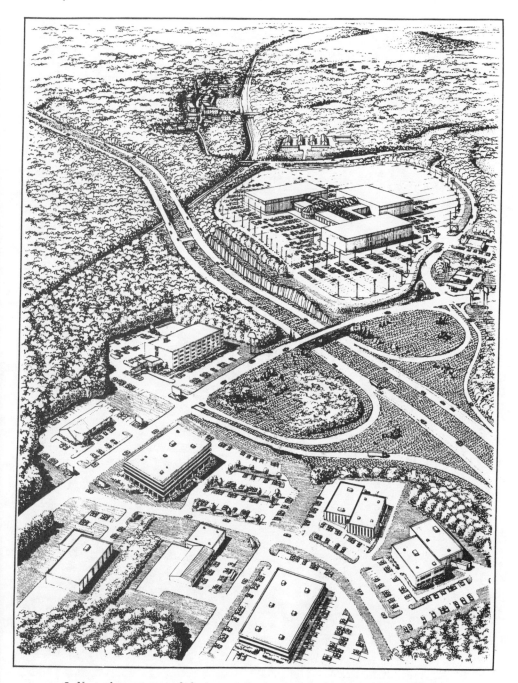

5. Next, the area around the intersection is zoned for business, and unplanned urban development takes place.

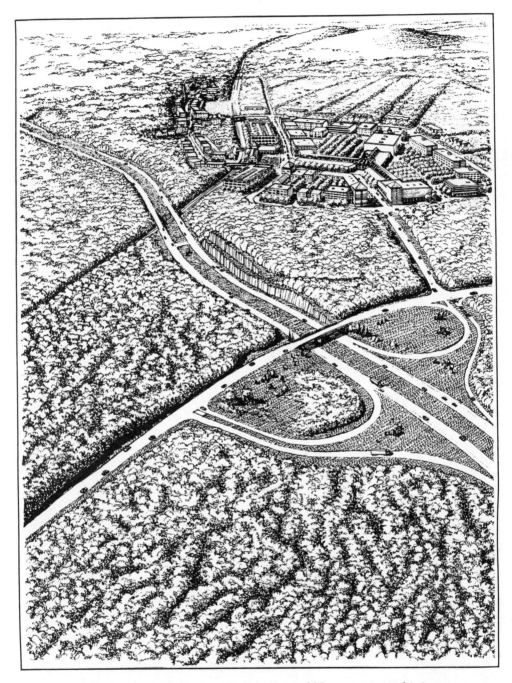

6. *If urbanization had been anticipated, zoning could have concentrated it in one quadrant of the interchange, close to an existing town.*

a cavalcade of cars takes everyone to the restaurant in yet another quadrant. The distances might be walkable, but no one should cross so many lanes of swiftly moving traffic, and the highway department usually puts up fences, in case anyone would be tempted to risk being a pedestrian.

If the investors and the community had understood that they were shaping several million square feet of urban development, they might well have preferred the alternative shown in the next drawing, concentrating new buildings in a single quadrant of the interchange nearest to an existing railway line and town, tying new investment to transportation and other communities. There would still be direct access from the highway, but the road would lead to a complete district containing office buildings, a hotel, and a shopping mall, all sharing landscaped parking courts.

Constructing such a compact urban center should be no more expensive than scattering the same structures over the landscape; and there would be savings in land and infrastructure costs. When it is as easy to walk from shopping to the hotel, or from the hotel to the offices as in a traditional downtown, the center can be served by public transportation. The accidental development around the interchange happened because conditions changed faster than either investors or government officials could figure out what was going on. Now that these new development forces are understood, they can be planned for in advance.

A second sequence of drawings [7, 8, 9] shows a typical strip of commercial buildings and parking along a highway, the way such a strip is likely to grow in the future, and a better alternative. In most suburbs the available business locations are all within these zoning strips, which continue to grow, wasting land and creating both an ugly environment and irreconcilable traffic conflicts.

A morning's errands might start with a trip from a residential neighborhood out to the strip to leave clothes at the dry cleaner's, followed by a mile-long drive down the strip to the hardware store, and then two miles in the other direction to the supermarket. In the meantime, other drivers are using the same highway to go from one town to another. Moving on and off the highway to reach local

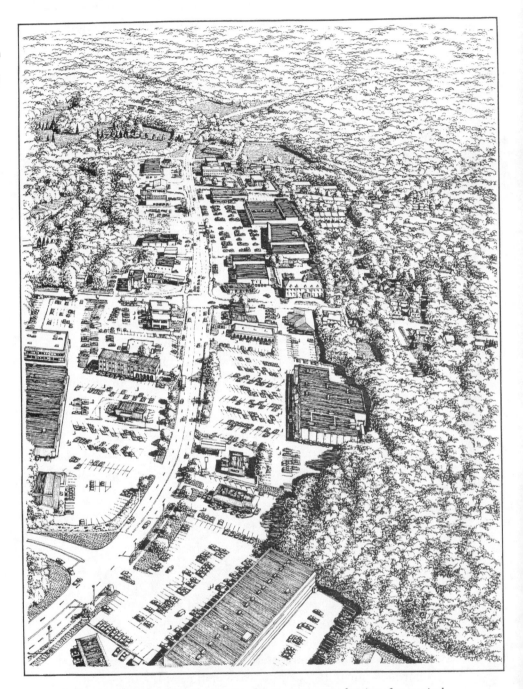

7. *Another Regional Plan Association drawing sequence showing, first, typical commercial development zoned in a strip along a suburban roadway.*

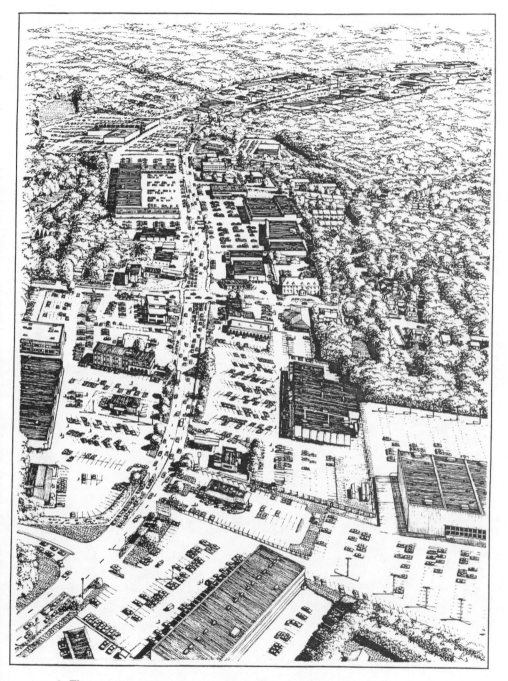

8. *The zoning permits continued extension of strip development.*

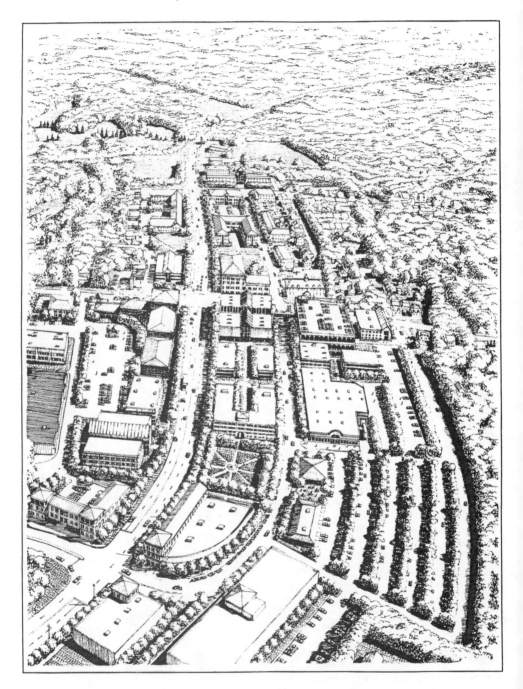

9. *Alternative zoning and urban redevelopment policies could turn parts of the commercial strip into town centers, other parts into residential districts. Illustrations 4–9 prepared for the Regional Plan Association, Robert Yaro, executive director, by Dodson Associates, Jonathan Barnett, consultant.*

businesses inevitably conflicts with through traffic, particularly when cars make midblock left turns from "suicide lanes" in the middle of the roadway.

In a traditional suburban downtown the same errands could be accomplished from a single parking space; in a traditional urban neighborhood all the errands could be done on foot.

The alternative to the strip, shown in the third drawing of the series, is to zone a few places for more concentrated development, supported by public parking garages and other investment incentives long understood in city centers but not yet much used in the suburbs. The drawing shows that zoning has been changed to match the surrounding area along segments of the highway where strip development has not yet taken place. Where commercial uses are to be phased out, the zoning has been changed to multifamily. Locations for town houses and garden apartments are often scarce in the suburbs, and can have an investment value comparable to that of low-density commercial districts. The apartments and town houses are shown facing the adjacent neighborhoods rather than the highway, which is landscaped to create a visual and acoustic buffer.

Having to drive to every destination and appointment precludes the variety of incident and the potential for casual contacts that traditionally have made downtown districts good business locations: the ability to set up a meeting on short notice, the chance to run into someone you know at lunch, the opportunity to shop on the way to and from work.

Suburban gridlock, with a short respite in midmorning before people go out to their lunchtime appointments and another brief interval in the afternoon before everyone starts heading home, is just the most obvious symptom of what is wrong with current development patterns. The high ratio of parking lots to buildings and the unwalkable distances across highways and service roads make it impossible to design any kind of architectural ensemble, while wasting land and raising infrastructure costs. Most important, because dispersed development patterns cannot be served by public transportation, additional buildings must then become even more dispersed to accommodate parking, making traffic problems even worse.

Compact development is thus an issue that goes beyond the design and experience of individual centers to affect the way everyone in a metropolitan region will live in the next few decades. Achieving compact development might require new kinds of suburban zoning districts on the analogy of the special mixed-use districts to be found in many urban downtowns. Cities routinely acquire blighted land for downtown redevelopment, a technique transferable to suburbs as the first generation of commercial development deteriorates. Another possibility is the specific plan, a zoning technique pioneered in California, which permits a local government to coordinate the development of an area divided among many different property owners. Skeptics may wonder whether such a public effort can be justified, even if compact centers fulfill transportation policy objectives and promote environmental conservation and improved infrastructure efficiency. There are significant economic advantages for individual investors from sharing parking spaces and thus reducing land and construction costs. Perhaps it is these advantages that will prove decisive.

Because each conventional suburban shopping center or office building is separate, each must satisfy its own parking requirement on its own property. A shopping center parking lot is filled only a few peak days, mostly weekends between Thanksgiving and Christmas. A typical parking requirement for a shopping center is 5 cars for every 1,000 square feet of store space. All that at-grade parking produces a ratio between the total area of the building and the total area of the property of about 0.33 to 1, compared to typical downtown zoning that permits the accommodation of floor space in tall buildings eight, ten, or fifteen times the area of the property. Parking requirements for shopping, the most urban of activities, ensure that it takes place in un-urban surroundings. Most of the time, most of this parking is not in use.

Over at the office park, at-grade parking for a typical 8-story office tower requires roughly ten times the land devoted to the building. On evenings and weekends, when the parking lot at the shopping center is filling up, the parking lots for the offices are almost deserted. The parking spaces for a hotel are mostly empty during the day, and could be used by both office workers and shoppers, if there were any nearby.

If it were possible to park in one place and walk from hotel to office building, and from office building to the mall, the land needed for parking could be reduced significantly, as spaces used by office workers during the day could be used by shoppers and hotel guests at night and on weekends. It might even be possible to save enough money on land and access roads to justify some structured parking, which could make the whole development still more compact and efficient. Overflow parking for peak days could be provided in peripheral areas, which in some climates might not even need to be paved. Because development is concentrated in a compact location, it could be served efficiently by a bus line, or even a rail rapid-transit system, making it possible to have even fewer car spaces.

Current zoning patterns of strips along highways and nodes around cloverleafs provide both too much land and too little space to encourage a compact alternative form of development. Too much land is zoned commercial to make it worthwhile for investors to investigate joint development with other entrepreneurs. At the same time, the extent of commercial zoning is sharply restricted to the vicinity of highways, so that sufficient commercially zoned space is rarely available at any one highway location to put offices, shops, and a hotel together the way they might be found in an older city center.

A map [10] prepared for a research project at the University of South Florida shows the existing zoning along the I-75 highway corridor as it bypasses Tampa, Florida. In theory these regulations permit something like 800 million square feet of development (more than twice the office space in all of Manhattan). A very optimistic estimate of actual development potential might be 80 million square feet over a twenty-five-year period. Because so much land has been allocated for high-density development, there is no incentive to use it well. For example, a proposed shopping center uses about one tenth the permitted density. If the zoning is not changed, it will produce the familiar fragmented pattern: an office park in one place, a shopping mall five miles away, and so on, all completely dependent on the automobile and each surrounded by vast parking fields.

The University of South Florida research team, not having to deal

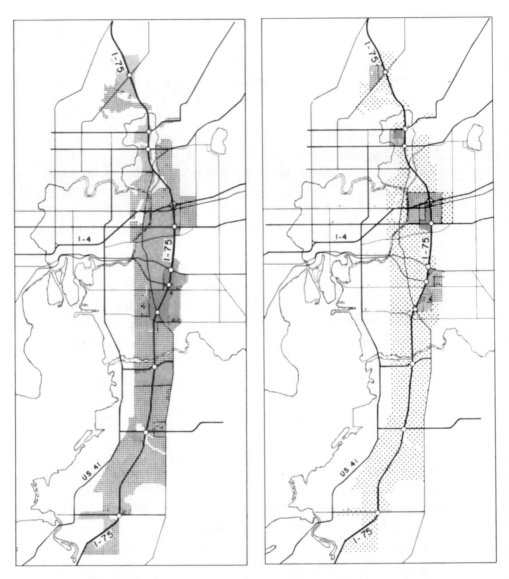

10. *Current zoning along the I-75 corridor east of Tampa, Florida, permits two and a half times the office space on Manhattan Island.*

11. *The alternative map shows development based on the most optimistic market projections concentrated in five major centers.*

with vocal land-owners demanding high-density zoning everywhere in the corridor, could produce an alternative regulatory map that accommodates optimistic growth projections in five compact locations, real urban areas that could be served by mass transit [11].

Compact development does not mean replicating early-twentieth-century downtowns. The enclosed shopping mall, for example, can be incorporated within a compact center. A design by Andres Duany and Elizabeth Plater-Zyberk for Avalon Park, a large planned community east of Orlando, Florida, takes a regional shopping mall with three department stores and assimilates it into the street pattern of the surrounding community [12]. Two of the three anchor stores are placed at the end of major streets; the third store faces a highway as in a conventional shopping center. An office tower is located to become a marker for the whole complex, which is ringed with smaller-scale multi-use buildings. Parking is shown as three car spaces per 1,000 square feet; overflow at peak times can be accommodated at curbside on the streets, or at remote locations. Diagrams prepared at the University of South Florida as part of the I-75 corridor study use these Avalon principles to show how a proposed shopping mall [13] could be transformed into the nucleus of a city center [14]; the drainage basins required by Florida environmental law are combined into an ornamental lake. When the shopping center is first built, the street pattern would be like the divisions in a conventional parking lot. Later office buildings could be added, sharing the parking, and then—as land values increase— parking garages would permit even more intense development along what would become city streets. Only then would the area begin to approach the kind of urban densities that have already been mapped for the highway corridor.

Some existing real estate developments can serve as models of compact suburban centers. One of the most interesting is the Reston Town Center in the Virginia suburbs of Washington, D.C. [15, 16]. Reston was planned in the early 1960s by the firm of Conklin and Rossant to follow Ebenezer Howard's model of a self-sufficient "garden city" surrounded by rural areas, and an urban center was part of the original plan. But by the time the architectural firm RTKL began designing this downtown, Reston had become an island of relative coherence in a sprawling urban corridor leading

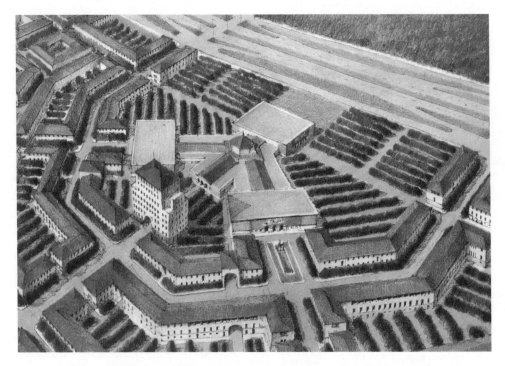

12. A proposal by Duany/Plater-Zyberk for Avalon Park, near Orlando, Florida, integrating a three-department-store shopping mall into a mixed-use center, equivalent to a traditional downtown.

13. A proposed shopping mall on I-75 near Tampa, Florida, uses about 10 percent of the permitted development rights.

14. An alternative proposal showing how a redesigned shopping mall could be the nucleus of a future urban center.

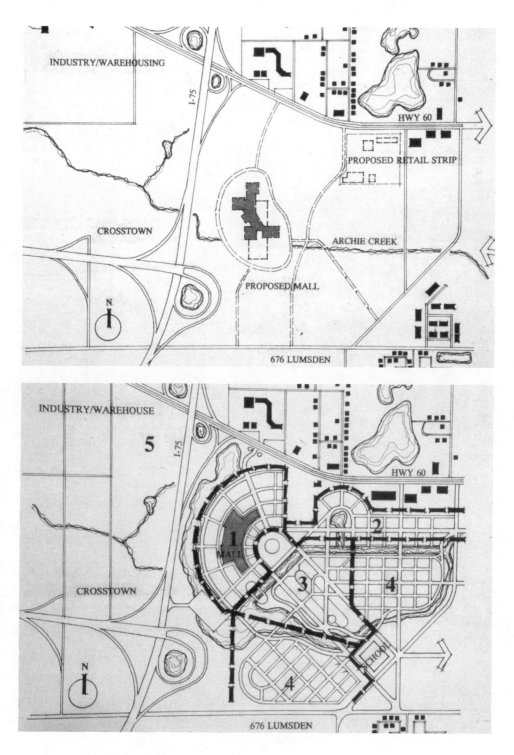

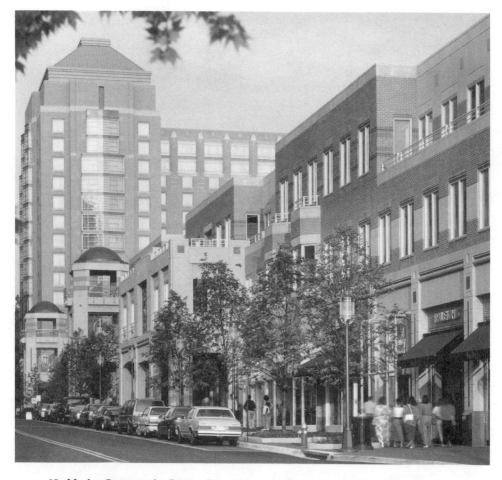

15. Market Street in the Reston Town Center: genuine urbanity, but right now surrounded by parking lots.

from Washington to Dulles Airport. The Reston Town Center is thus just another development in western Fairfax County, and not a realization of Howard's regional planning theories. The design does, however, achieve the compact urban character that makes it a suitable hub for a modern garden city. The first phase of the center combines 550,000 square feet of offices, 200,000 square feet of retail, 11 film theaters, and a 500-room hotel, all organized in blocks, much like a traditional downtown. The retail is at street level with circulation along Market Street and Fountain Square, not along an internal mall (although there are midblock concourses with shop frontages). Right now, the Reston Center looks like a city

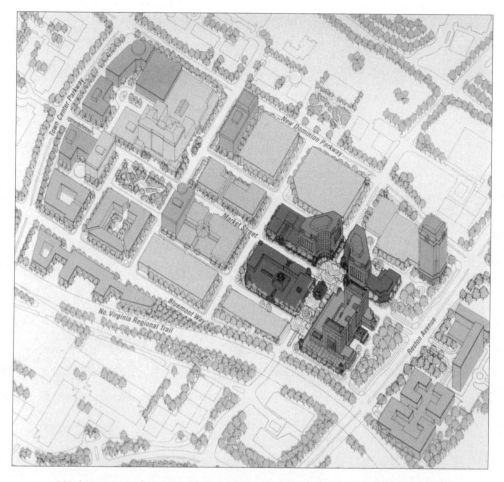

16. *Axonometric drawing of Reston Town Center as it will look when completed; the buildings with the darker tone are already built. The master plan and first buildings are by the architectural firm RTKL.*

only when you walk or drive up Market Street; if you drive around the periphery of the four completed blocks you are still looking at an island of buildings surrounded by parking. Ultimately, however, these parking spaces become blocks housing another 100,000 square feet of shopping, close to 2,000,000 additional square feet of office space, another 700 hotel rooms, plus 600 to 800 apartments. Completion of this program would confirm that real city blocks, storefronts, and a traditional mix of uses are a marketable alternative to accidental suburban development around highway interchanges.

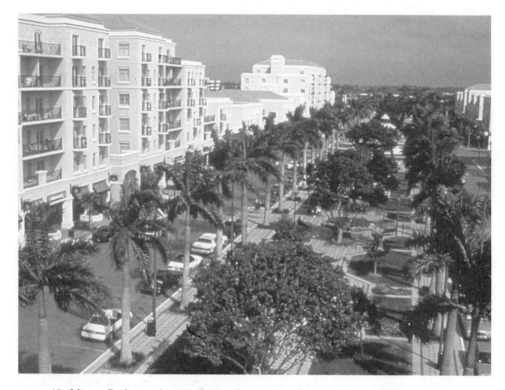

17. *Mizner Park is a shopping center designed by Cooper, Carry and Associates along a two-block grand boulevard instead of as an enclosed mall. Upper floors are occupied by offices and apartments.*

If the Reston Town Center right now is an office park themed as a downtown, Mizner Park in Boca Raton, Florida, is a shopping center whose theme is a grand boulevard in a city center [17, 18, 19]. It replaced a failed 20-year-old conventional regional shopping mall in downtown Boca Raton, an area that was much more like a suburban commercial strip strung out along U.S. Highway 1 than a traditional city center. The city's Community Renewal Agency purchased the site and advertised for development proposals. The development, designed by Cooper, Carry & Associates, is a private street with a park running down the center. The street is lined with arcaded shops. The upper floors on one side are apartment buildings and across the street are offices. Right now this grand boulevard is only two blocks long, and it remains to be seen whether its somewhat schematic mix of uses will eventually become the core of a larger downtown. It does demonstrate, however, that a compact

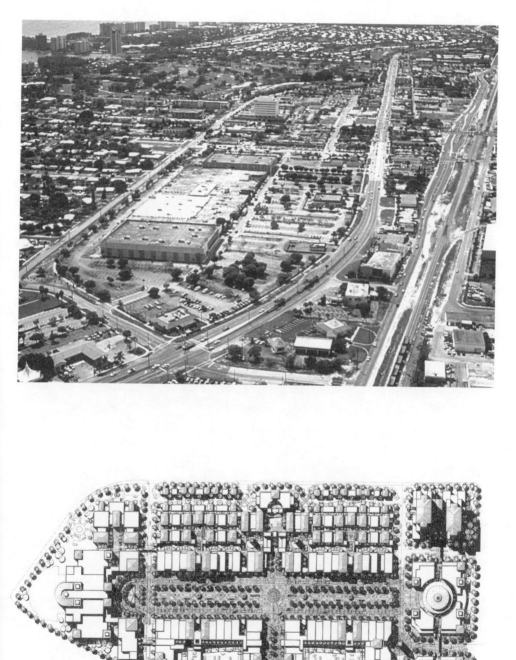

18. *The site of Mizner Park was a failed shopping center in downtown Boca Raton.*

19. *Map showing Mizner Park as part of a future downtown district.*

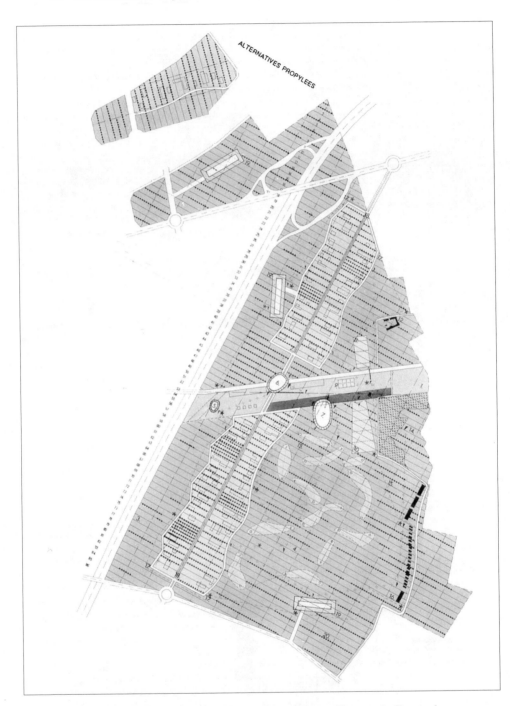

20. *A strip commercial and industrial development near Chartres, in France, has been designed by Bernard Tschumi to be enclosed within a park.*

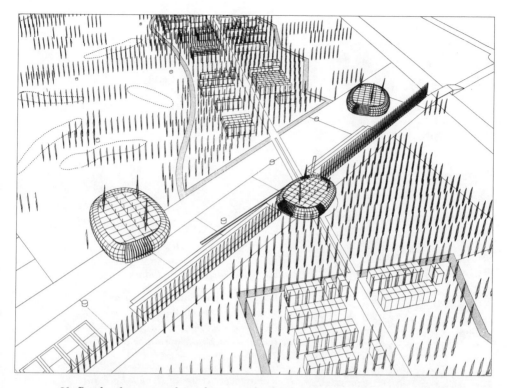

21. *Bands of trees are planned to cross the development on a diagonal, creating a formal order that cannot be created by the buildings.*

center with stores, offices, and apartments can be a successful real estate investment.

Another possible model that responds directly to the problems of creating urbanity with standard suburban ingredients is the design by Bernard Tschumi for an office and industrial park near Chartres in France. Tschumi accepts that the main street of the development is going to be lined with a random collection of buildings of different sizes, built at different times in an unpredictable order. As in most suburban development, there is so much parking for each building that it is unlikely that the buildings can form architectural relationships with each other. Instead, he isolates the strip development within a park, so that the surrounding greenspace dominates the commercial development [20]. His design then calls for parallel rows of trees that march from the park across the parking lots of the development [21]. The strip is also broken into two by a sports park

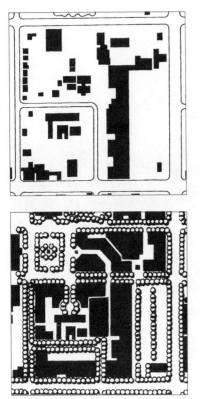

22. *A figure-ground drawing showing development at a major intersection along Park Boulevard in Pinellas Park, Florida.*

23. *A figure-ground drawing of projected redevelopment of the same area shown at left, using existing strip shopping as the nucleus of a new center, as proposed by Hansen and Taylor and Jonathan Barnett.*

24. *A convenience center at Avalon Park, a design by Duany/Plater-Zyberk.*

that crosses it on a diagonal, the diagonal based on a distant view of Chartres Cathedral. The design absolutely must have the trees in order to work. If the trees are planted in the orderly rows shown, they will subdue and organize the random buildings and parking, demonstrating that new development in suburbs need not be designed to look like traditional cities; it just needs to be designed.

Long stretches of commercial-strip shopping districts can also be redesigned, if communities are willing to adopt new zoning policies. A strategy similar to that described in the Regional Plan Association diagram [9] is being implemented by the city of Pinellas Park, Florida. Instead of continuous commercial zoning, the plan restricts commercial development to important locations and remaps the rest of the strip to a special mixed-use district for garden apartments or town houses, with possible ground-floor office or commercial space. An existing strip shopping center has been identified as the nucleus of a new, much more concentrated civic and commercial

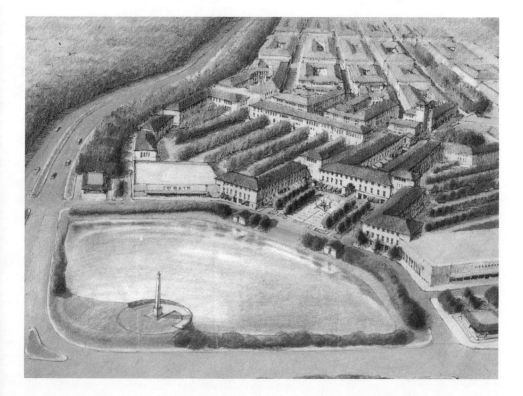

district. The figure-ground plans [22, 23] show how the existing widely spaced, scattered buildings can be pulled together into a more coherent street and block pattern.

Illustration 24 shows a neighborhood commercial district at Avalon Park, Florida, the planned community designed by Duany and Plater-Zyberk that is also the location for the regional center shown in Illustration 12. The neighborhood center has both a grocery and a drug store, each designed at the new suburban scale that puts more than 50,000 square feet of retail space under one roof, plus other related shops at street level, with offices or apartments above. The Avalon plan also includes other local convenience shopping and smaller neighborhood centers. The parking ratio at each of these centers is three cars per 1,000 square feet of shops—a reduction from the more usual five-car standard—made possible by close integration with the surrounding areas. All are designed with rows of trees separating the parking bays.

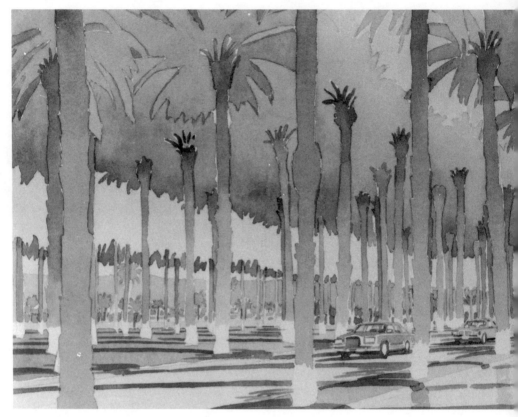

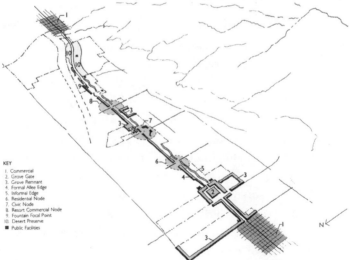

KEY
1. Commercial
2. Grove Gate
3. Grove Remnant
4. Formal Allee Edge
5. Informal Edge
6. Residential Node
7. Civic Node
8. Resort Commercial Node
9. Fountain Focal Point
10. Desert Preserve
■ Public Facilities

25. *Perspective of a landscaped alternative to strip development along Highway 111, Indian Wells, California.*

26. *A schematic plan of the Highway 111 corridor, Indian Wells, California, designed by Johnson, Fain & Pereira Associates, Jonathan Barnett, consultant.*

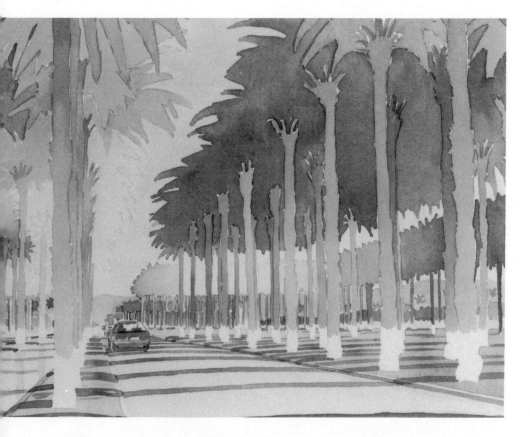

Highway 111 in Indian Wells, California, was never zoned or developed as a commercial strip, but land along the highway was held vacant, and the owners may well have expected to build typical highway-related businesses someday. Instead, Indian Wells decided to confine commercial development within two concentrated areas where the highway entered and left the community, and to landscape the rest of the highway corridor. Instead of being zoned commercial, land along the highway was mapped for resort development or multifamily housing. Substantial landscaped setbacks are required along the highway; the owners may transfer the development rights for the land within the setbacks to sites farther from the right of way. The plan, by Johnson Fain & Pereira Associates, placed a grove of date palms at the northern entrance to the community. Some of the trees are being transplanted from a nearby plantation that is going to be redeveloped. Cars pass through the grove and enter a landscaped boulevard [25, 26] with formal rows of date palms along one side and more informal landscaping on the other, which permits views of the mountains. Specific locations along the highway, such as the city hall, are given their own landscaped character. The landscaping also incorporates berms and plantings to reduce the transmission of highway noise to the neighborhoods on either side of the highway. At the southern end of the highway, a small portion of natural desert landscape has been preserved, giving drivers a different experience. The highway, instead of dividing the community into two parts, or being a congested, ugly and inefficient commercial strip, becomes a connecting element, an experience that defines the community and holds it together.

In *Edge City*, Joel Garreau lists 123 new urban developments in North America (four in the Toronto metropolitan area, the rest in the U.S). In Garreau's definition an Edge City has 5 million leasable square feet of office space or more, and thus is clearly an employment center, has at least 600,000 square feet of retail space of a type that makes the area a destination, and is located in a place that 30 years ago was overwhelmingly residential or rural in character. According to Garreau there are another seventy-eight incipient Edge Cities (five near Toronto). Garreau's list is not intended to be exhaustive and includes Old-Town Alexandria, Virginia, which has a strong, historic fabric; planned developments like Columbia, Maryland, and the Research Triangle in North Carolina; plus some urban districts supported by mass transit, like Crystal City and Ballston in Arlington County, Virginia. But most of the places Garreau calls Edge Cities have the accidental character described in Illustration 5: each building has its own separate parking lot, walking from place to place is nearly impossible, and the relationship of one building to the next is purely a product of circumstance. Can anything be done to improve these places?

Local governments already have the power to make incipient or future Edge Cities into something much more like the Avalon or Reston town centers through zoning and development incentives. What has been missing until recently has been an understanding of development forces, plus the political will to take charge of the community's future. Intervention in existing areas of fragmented Edge City development is much more difficult, requiring either reconstruction, which needs an economic justification for tearing down relatively new buildings, or replacement of parking lots with garages, which frees infill sites for development but may raise densities beyond the capacity of the transportation system.

Tyson's Corner, Virginia, the Irvine business center in California, and the Parkway Center district in suburban north Dallas are all accidental cities that have recently been the subject of urban design studies seeking ways to transform them into more workable and livable places.

Tyson's Corner is perhaps the most famous of all Edge Cities and one of the most accidental. It has two massive regional shopping centers right across the street from each other; not only is it nearly impossible to walk from one to the other, it isn't easy to drive between them either. There are currently more than 15 million square feet of office space, mostly in isolated individual buildings with separate parking lots, plus 3,000 hotel rooms and 2,500 apartments.

The proposals for Tyson's Corner, by the landscape architecture firm EDAW, associated with the architectural firm ADD, Inc., included an internal transportation link-up, a public open space system, and four relatively small areas of infill that could be more concentrated village centers. A more ambitious plan to create building patterns similar to a city center at Tyson's would mean a massive increase in density, which is currently beyond the capacity of the local transportation system.

Building patterns similar to a city center were proposed at Irvine, in a plan by the firms of HOK and Sasaki Associates requiring both reconstruction and infill, but the plan proved too controversial and has been withdrawn for further study.

The proposals in Dallas by Barton, Aschman Associates and Sasaki Associates are directed toward making property owners realize that they are part of a district that can be identified, linked by transportation and open space, and added to in a coherent way. As at Tyson's Corner, the plan is based on a secondary transit system that links potential areas of more concentrated development.

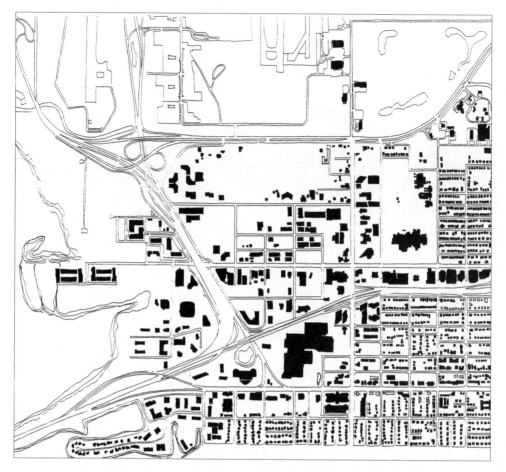

27. *A figure-ground plan of existing development in the Westshore area of Tampa, Florida.*

28. *An alternative figure-ground plan showing proposals for future development of Westshore with streets restored and a shopping mall connecting the two parts of the area after the highway has been raised and widened by the state. Plan developed by a Master's Studio at the University of South Florida School of Architecture, James Moore and Jonathan Barnett, studio critics.*

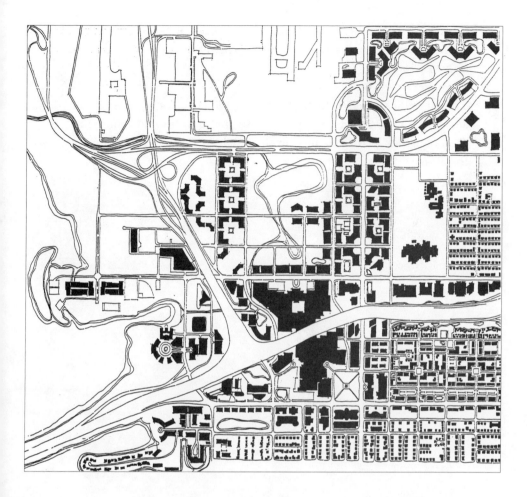

Another research project at the University of South Florida took official growth projections for the Westshore area of Tampa and demonstrated how new buildings could be added to the scattered development already there to create a real urban center [27, 28]. The expressway that bisects the Westshore region is being raised and rebuilt in a wider configuration. While the highway will be much more intrusive than it is now, raising it permits more through street connections and also creates an opportunity to extend the Westshore Mall under the highway and link it with a second regional mall to the north. The result would be a shopping center where people could enter a retail concourse on one side of the highway and emerge from a door at the other end, without being aware of the highway at all. Restoring the underlying street and block system and adding residential development would also help to make Westshore more of an urban center, with densities that support rapid transit and where people can walk from one destination to another.

These studies are small steps toward ex post facto redesign of accidental cities. More comprehensive methods should emerge as designers look at these places, evaluate what exists, and invent ways to improve them.

3

Suburban Sprawl:
Its Prevention and Cure

I
t takes years of meticulous engineering and months of public
hearings and approvals before a hillside can be bulldozed into
a parking lot, or a highway lined with drive-ins and billboards.
The result is so ubiquitous, and so familiar, that people assume that
it must be the work of powerful economic forces. But what has
directed the new urbanization up to now is not so much the invisible
hand of the marketplace as the deadly grip of outmoded regulations.

The planners and good-government advocates who struggled for
decades to make sure new development followed zoning and subdivision controls have won their battle, but by the time all communities had finally adopted these ordinances, the models on which
they were based had become obsolete. Planning boards and local
governments are trying to direct today's regional shopping malls, or
office parks with millions of square feet of space, or new developments with thousands of houses, using regulations invented two
generations ago for city neighborhoods or for making modest additions to separate small towns and residential suburbs.

The commercial strip as a zoning artifact is derived from real estate
patterns in one-main-street towns, and later from the continuous
shopping frontages that developed along streetcar routes through
urban neighborhoods. This 1920s real estate pattern was built into
the thousands of suburban ordinances enacted in the 1950s; appar-
ently no one stopped to contemplate the effect of mapping commercial land exclusively in narrow strips along highways where the only
means of access was the automobile.

The sameness that so many people complain about in suburban
housing has also been created by obsolete legislation. The land is

leveled, and the natural landscape stripped away in the process, to meet grading standards for streets required by the subdivision ordinance. The property is then divided into lots of similar size, and the houses are all set back from the edges of the lots for similar distances, as required by the zoning ordinance.

These regulations were invented to fit relatively small increments of new development into towns and cities that were already well established. It was not anticipated that lot-by-lot zoning and subdivision would become the sole development control for hundreds or even thousands of acres, as has now become routine. The requirements are blind to the idiosyncrasies of terrain and orientation, the beauties of the natural landscape, the perils of erosion and ecological disturbance. They say nothing about variety, balance, or the necessary ingredients of a community. At a small scale, within established towns or suburbs, these deficiencies were not severe; but conventional zoning and subdivision are disastrously inadequate when used to create whole new residential areas.

Large lot zoning applied uniformly over the landscape, interspersed with strip commercial zones along highways, is the recipe for urban sprawl; and sprawl will continue as long as these regulations remain in force.

Local officials have been aware for years that they need better ways to manage growth, but until recently the best way to overcome the deficiencies of local zoning and subdivision ordinances has been planned unit development, sometimes known as cluster zoning. It is an improvement over old-style land subdivision and site engineering, because a design that relates buildings to the landscape replaces an abstract pattern of standard streets, lots, and setbacks. Planned unit development amendments to zoning ordinances can help protect the most environmentally sensitive areas and ease some of the most unreasonable regulatory restrictions for large projects. But experience has created disenchantment with planned unit development, a useful procedure, but not the cure-all it was once thought to be. Clustering buildings does not correct the underlying defects of commercial strips or extensive tracts of large-lot zoning. The looser regulations possible within planned unit development apply only to large tracts of unbuilt land. Developers are encouraged to

look for properties at the fringe of communities, which both acceler-
ates urban sprawl and—by making it easier to build elsewhere—
allows developers to skip more difficult infill sites that ought to be
developed first.

Planned unit development also encourages the creation of isolated
districts with separate street systems, which fragment communities
socially and cause more traffic congestion than in traditionally
planned towns and suburbs with more alternate routes.

The most serious difficulty with planned unit development is its
tendency to reduce all regulation to a negotiated deal between the
developer and the planning authorities. Most planned unit development approvals require the same procedure used for a change in
zoning. Without additional time and effort a developer can seek less
strict land-use controls and higher densities while requesting the
relatively minor modifications to the setback and street-mapping
constraints customary under planned unit development. The proposed design, plus big increases in the development permitted by
the underlying zoning, are presented in one sophisticated and often
misleading package. As metropolitan areas have grown to include
small towns and unincorporated parts of counties, local authorities
are often outgunned by the developer's planning and legal team.

Local governments can charge the developer a fee for processing the
application and then retain the necessary legal, engineering, and
planning advice, but the psychology of the situation now favors the
developer. Having paid up-front, the developer appears to be entitled to at least some of what is applied for, even if the proposal raises
serious problems for the community.

Charging developers a fee to cover professional advice opens the
door to other exactions. Why not make the developer of a shopping
center pay for the necessary road widenings and new traffic signals?
What about assistance in completing a new sewage treatment plant?
A new school?

As communities develop a history of negotiated zoning in return for
developer payments, developers who do not get all they ask for are
more likely to go to court, accusing the community of not applying

the zoning law fairly. Defending a lawsuit can be an intimidating prospect for a small community that does not have the in-house law department of a big city or metropolitan county. A few days of depositions taken by big-city lawyers making unpleasant insinuations may be enough to cause a town to give way and settle. Matching the developer in the courtroom is an expensive, uncertain, long-term effort, with a painfully unsettling effect on the tax base as well as on the emotional equilibrium of volunteer planning board and town council members.

Negotiated zoning in developing areas thus runs the risk of deteriorating into no zoning at all. The alternative is for everyone to operate on automatic pilot. The developer and builder follow outmoded zoning and subdivision requirements, and thus have little control over many basic design decisions. The planning board and local political leaders have little control either. They have to enforce the regulations on the books.

The resulting frustration often makes local decision-making an acrimonious process. To some citizens, any new development will be worse than no development at all, while developers either have to commit to options or land purchases while waiting out a seemingly endless series of hearings and reviews, or proceed with cookie-cutter projects. Thoughtful members of planning boards and community councils, who give up many of their evenings for meetings, often get more abuse than praise for their efforts.

It is depressing to contemplate how much bad development has been caused by faulty public policies, but communities are beginning to realize that they can revise their codes and reassert control over their own future. Two important ways to limit suburban sprawl are environmental zoning ordinances and local growth boundaries. Environmental zoning can be adopted independently by any community; growth boundaries work best when mandated by state planning laws so that neighboring communities must coordinate their regulations.

Conventional development regulation defines land as a commodity, to be allocated into zones for various uses. The landscape becomes a Monopoly board criss-crossed by invisible district lines, each with its permitted use and density. But land is actually an ecosystem, a set of fragile interrelationships among soils and vegetation, water, and contour.

In the past, the idiosyncrasies of landscape were seen as engineering problems: swamps were to be drained, streams restricted to culverts, hillsides leveled, and land stripped and regraded so that streets did not exceed a slope of 5 or 6 percent.

Skillful engineering could recontour any landscape. In time, new trees and shrubs would grow (although not in parking lots or along highways in business zones), and the land would settle into a typical urban or suburban pattern.

The scale of urbanization that began in the 1960s raised questions about development engineering. What was acceptable editing of nature when done in selected areas had serious negative consequences when applied to the natural landscape for hundreds of square miles, particularly as cities grew together to form chains of urbanized areas, such as the megalopolis that extends along the U.S. East Coast from Portland, Maine, to Richmond, Virginia.

Natural drainage systems are being changed in whole regions, creating erosion and flash flooding. The runoff from parking lots, septic tanks, and garden fertilizer is polluting watersheds and aquifers. Drinking water is being piped in from greater and greater distances. As development becomes more dispersed, automobile and industrial pollution are spreading over larger areas.

Development in some places may already be unsustainable. Any metropolitan area that is withdrawing water from underground aquifers faster than they can recharge puts the future of the whole region in question. Similarly, a barrier beach covered with houses on small lots is an unstable development pattern. It is natural for barrier beaches to shift and erode, although unpleasant for the individual home owner, whose life may be in danger during a big storm, and who may well see a substantial investment swept out to sea. Grass fires can move swiftly across semiarid hillsides, part of a natural cycle and not a major problem—unless houses have been built there. Floods along streams and rivers can be controlled by dams, levees, and channels, but some places are so flood-prone they should not be developed.

Urbanization has also reached the point where withdrawing more land from natural systems can cause sweeping ecological changes, with incalculable long-range effects. Filling and draining coastal wetlands, once routine development practice, are now understood to affect the development of all marine life in the area and, by disturbing bird migrations, also affect the ecological balance of distant places.

Since the National Environmental Policy Act was passed in 1969 a new federal and state regulatory system has grown up that parallels local zoning and subdivision ordinances and often contradicts them. There is legislation directed at specific environmental problems and legislation requiring environmental impact analysis for individual projects.

At the federal level there is now a portfolio of specific environmental laws, and the bureaucracies to administer them. New buildings in flood-plain areas are effectively uninsurable if they don't meet the requirements of the Federal Emergency Management Agency. The states are required by the Federal Coastal Zone Management law to provide further regulatory protection for ecologically sensitive coastal areas. The Clean Air Act sets regional air quality standards. Communities in violation can lose federal funding. Standards are still being phased in, so that relatively few people understand what a powerful development control this act could be. Among the other specific federal environmental regulations are laws protecting endangered species and setting requirements for water quality.

The National Environmental Policy Act (known as NEPA) and the similar state laws requiring environmental impact statements were not expected to be powerful regulatory tools. The original intent was to make sure that sponsors of major projects using federal funds or affecting large areas of a state did their homework before starting construction. The laws say nothing about acceptable or unacceptable impacts; they simply ask for a comprehensive analysis of potential environmental and social consequences, and the interactions among them, before a project is permitted to proceed. Courts have now given ordinary citizens, as participants in the environment, standing to challenge the adequacy of environmental impact statements, giving NEPA and similar state legislation a kind of backhanded regulatory power.

Note that the challenge must be to the way the statement has been drafted, not to whether various impacts make approving a project good or bad public policy. The documents have consequently become more and more detailed and voluminous, and thus ever more expensive, in an attempt to make them lawsuit-proof. The regulatory effect comes from developers avoiding wherever possible any action requiring substantial documentation, whatever its merits.

The interaction of federal and state environmental regulation with local zoning and subdivision has created an amazingly complex regulatory tangle, which is frustrating to everyone and is not producing the favorable results to be expected from so much time and effort. It would be more logical for the zoning and environmental regulation for a region to agree, rather than having one kind of development mapped in the zoning ordinance, and quite another emerge from hearings before the Coastal Zone Management Commission. There ought to be a way of defining acceptable environmental impacts for whole regions in advance, just as conventional zoning defines acceptable land use and density in advance.

The carrying capacity of land is a measurement that goes a long way toward defining acceptable environmental impact. The carrying capacity of tidal wetlands, for example, is close to 0, as even a road will alter the movement of water and interfere with delicate ecological processes. On the other hand, a level, well-drained meadow may have a carrying capacity of close to 100 percent.

Between tidal wetlands and upland meadows is a range of classifications. The steeper the hillside, the lower its carrying capacity, as construction destabilizes the natural equilibrium. News accounts of houses subsiding in mudslides are extreme examples; most often the damage is less visible, but not necessarily less significant, taking the form of erosion of topsoil and vegetation, settlement cracks in walls and ceilings, and water flowing through the basement. River

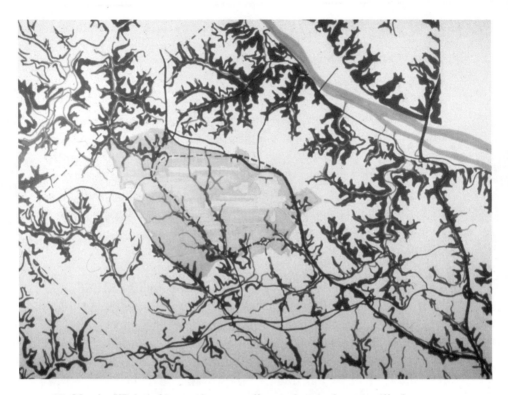

29. *Map by UDA Architects of stream valleys and steep slopes in Allegheny County around the Pittsburgh airport.*

edges, ravines, and other areas that become watercourses during major storms or snow-melts also have limited carrying capacity, as obstructing floodways will cause water to flow into areas that would otherwise remain dry. Trees and other vegetation are important for landscape stability, sheltering wildlife and moderating ambient temperature. Mature woodlands, which take a long time to replace, should have a lower carrying capacity rating than open areas, although the slope of the land is also a factor in determining the importance of vegetation. Certain types of soil are more prone to erosion than others, and subsurface bearing conditions should always be investigated.

The book *Design with Nature*, by Ian McHarg, originally published in 1969 and recently reissued, has done the most to popularize carrying capacity as a necessary part of land-use planning. McHarg's theories were translated into zoning methodology by Lane Kendig,

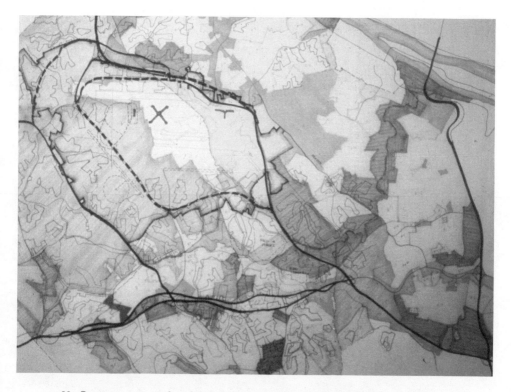

30. *Current commercial and industrial zoning in Allegheny County tends to be in strips along highways, and the highways follow the stream valleys.*

who describes his approach in a book entitled *Performance Zoning,* which was first published in 1980.

McHarg analyzes environmental constraints on land planning by making a series of maps on transparent overlays. Each category of ecological sensitivity is described on a separate overlay; the areas free of any mapped constraint are the places most appropriate for development. The map [29] prepared by UDA Architects shows the result of such an analysis for the four-township region surrounding the Greater Pittsburgh International Airport in Allegheny County, Pennsylvania. As often happens, the most sensitive areas are all part of a connected geologic pattern, in this case created by streams cutting through a plateau as they flow into the Ohio River. The best area to build is the generally flat plateau.

If you compare the environmental map with a map showing the

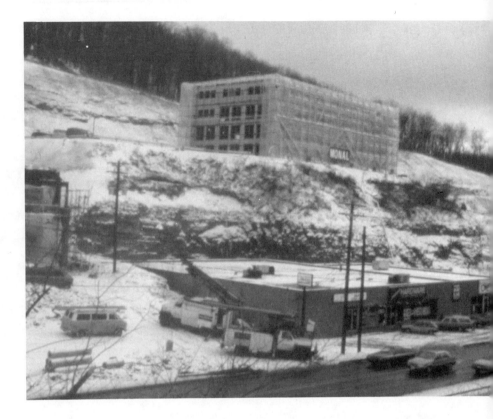

location of commercial and industrial zones in the four townships
[30], most of the highest intensity zoning turns out to be within the
watershed areas that are least suitable for construction. The first
roads in the district were built next to streams, as the road builders
followed the easiest gradient. The roads themselves are not a serious
environmental problem; the damage is caused by the strip commercial and industrial zones mapped along them.

The photographs [31, 32] taken in another part of Allegheny
County with similar terrain show the disastrous environmental effect of strip commercial zoning along a road that goes through a
narrow valley. The first generation of development is squeezed up
against the road by the steep topography on either side; the hillside
has actually been cut away, making erosion almost inevitable. The
second generation of development, a substantial office building, is
"benched" halfway up the hillside, with a second benched area for
its parking lot. Engineering makes this construction possible; but
it is strip commercial zoning that makes it necessary.

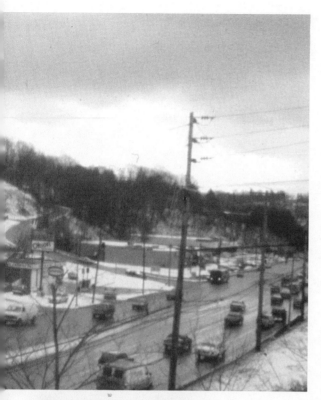

31. Buildings in a commercial
zone mapped along a highway
that follows a stream bed have to
be constructed on terrain that is
not suitable for development.

32. The rear of the roadside
building in the preceding
illustration. Treating natural
systems this way invites
appropriate retribution.

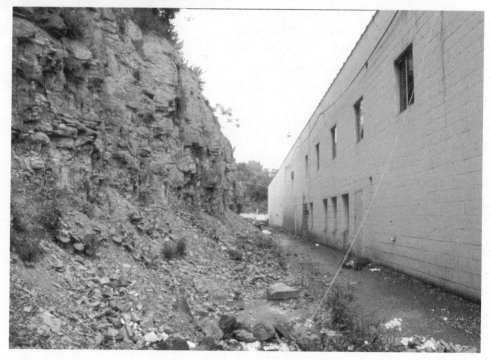

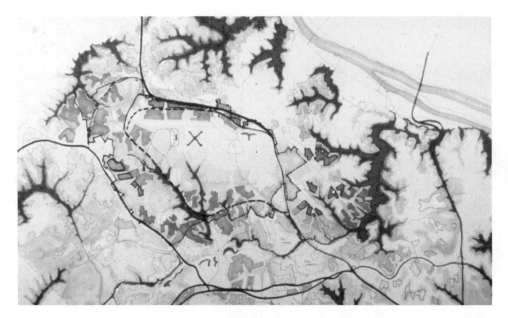

33. *Proposed zoning map by UDA Architects for the same area as shown in Illustration 30, with development locations based on environmental considerations, plus noise zones related to the airport.*

Where such development belongs is up on the plateau, as shown in the proposed zoning map [33], not halfway down a steep slope. A single building on a steep slope may not in itself have much effect on the environment, but zoning that mandates the continued development of such sensitive areas is clearly a mistake.

While preventing flooding and erosion are the most obvious reasons for preserving the existing landscape, other more subtle, aesthetic issues are also important. Landscape can become part of a region's culture, just as historic buildings do, and loss of familiar landscapes is one of the most frequent regrets voiced about new development. Growth and change will always alter landscape, just as new development in an existing downtown requires demolition of older structures. But just as cities have learned ways of preserving historic districts, buildings, and facades, it is possible to preserve significant natural features.

Illustrations 34 and 35, prepared by the Center for Rural Massachu-

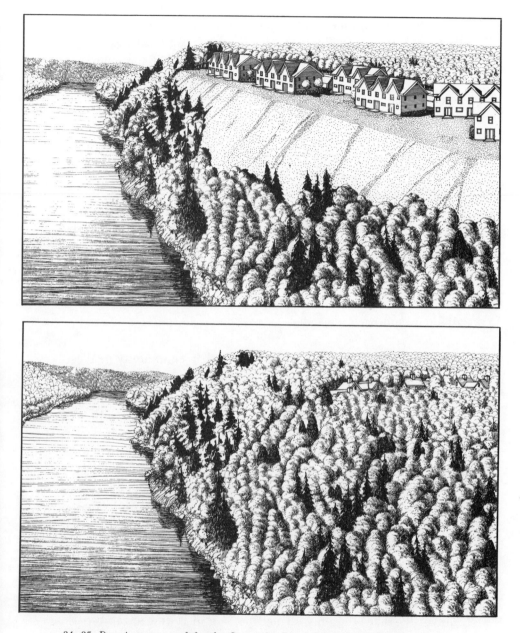

34, 35. Drawings prepared for the Center for Rural Massachusetts show new garden apartments on a bluff overlooking a river, first following conventional development practice, and then as they might appear if the community had a tree preservation ordinance, modified the grading requirements in the subdivision ordinance, and used site plan approval under planned unit development zoning to keep buildings away from the edge of the bluff.

setts, demonstrate how equal amounts of development can either destroy the scenic qualities of a landscape or can be absorbed into the existing landscape pattern. The destruction of the landscape shown in the first example is all too familiar, and almost inevitable under most local ordinances. How can communities change the rules?

In a planned unit development the amount of new building permitted is customarily computed as if the site had no topographical irregularities or environmentally sensitive areas. This theoretical density is then transferred to the most buildable portions of the site, often too small for the building allocated to it—or perhaps the developer doesn't own the place where new development would be most appropriate. Assuming the surface of a billiard table as the ideal for a development site comes from defining land primarily as a commodity and not an ecosystem. To preserve the ecosystem a different approach is needed.

The planning board of Irvington, a suburban community in Westchester County near New York City, had struggled valiantly with several new planned unit developments, but the loss of familiar landscapes and the appearance of the new buildings were both very unpopular. As in most suburban communities, no one had ever thought of Irvington's development regulations as a picture of what the community would one day become. Zoning and subdivision were abstract directives, covering any number of possibilities. But given the current rate of new construction, it looked as if Irvington could develop completely in the current residents' lifetimes, rather than in some indefinite future. As demand for land continued, open space the community had taken for granted would come under increasing development pressure. The wooded hillsides around the reservoir were privately owned; another big estate belonged to a university that used only a small portion of it as a research park. And what about the country club? Or what about all the oversize lots? When people retire and move to a warmer climate, they could subdivide their property and increase its value.

The community was going to have to consider changes in the development regulations to save the qualities that were attracting development in the first place. Irvington decided to modify its zoning ordinance to incorporate the environmental principles articulated by Ian McHarg, as translated into zoning methods by Lane Kendig.

Two maps [36, 37] show the western part of Irvington at the time of the study, compared to the same area as it could develop under the regulations then in force. Permitted amounts of building were computed using the "billiard table" theory, and then designed as well as possible. Irvington does not turn into a lunar landscape in these projections; it ends up looking like ordinary suburbia. But that is the point: much of the community's individual character has been erased. Wooded hillsides have turned into building lots. The great meadow that had been a scenic feature of the community for generations has disappeared into a pattern of streets and houses. Mature trees have had to be cut down to meet the grading requirements for new lots and streets. Like so much of suburbia, everything looks the same, a uniform carpet of development everywhere.

Compare this conventional build-out with the third map [38], illustrating the effect of relating zoning density to the carrying capacity of the land. The village is fully developed, but the meadow is still there, and the vista from the meadow to the Hudson has been preserved. The next maps show the whole Village of Irvington as it was at the beginning of the study [39] and a public open space plan that shows how existing parks, and the ecologically sensitive open spaces preserved through zoning, have been joined into a coherent park system—based largely on natural ecological patterns—providing a permanent landscape setting for the community [40]. The underlying zones have been modified only slightly, but, instead of theoretical "billiard table" computations, permitted development on an individual site is discounted from the mapped zoning in proportion to the carrying capacity or scenic value of the land. For example, Lane Kendig suggests that a portion of the site that is actually under water would be discounted 100 percent, shoreline areas 75 percent, mature woodlands 85 percent, slopes of 15 degrees or greater 70 percent, and so on. A developer applying for a building permit must present, as part of the application, a site map showing all natural features, with contours described at two-foot intervals. Areas of environmental sensitivity are computed, discounted, and the discounts subtracted from the overall site area. As the site area is the basis for development potential in all zoning

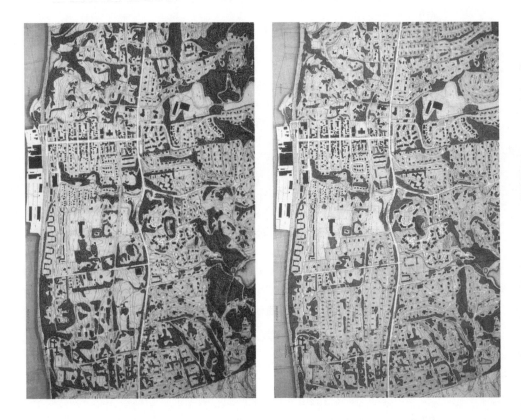

districts, this single amendment to the zoning applies to the whole community. The zoning is backed up by a tree preservation ordinance and a grading ordinance, to ensure that developers can't strip and regrade a property before seeking development approval. The subdivision ordinance has also been revised to make it easier for the community to acquire preserved outdoor open space for public use.

New York State requires environmental impact statements for significant new projects. While Irvington's environmental zoning (which itself required an impact statement before it was adopted) does not cover all the issues that come up in an environmental impact analysis, it eliminates most of the conflicts that are commonly found between permitted development and adverse environmental impacts. Complying with the zoning thus assures a high level of compatibility with the existing environment and simplifies the regulatory process.

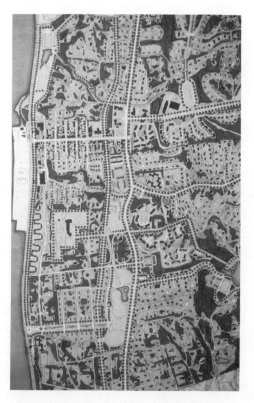

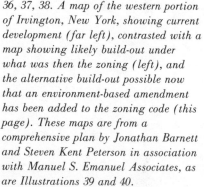

36, 37, 38. A map of the western portion of Irvington, New York, showing current development (far left), contrasted with a map showing likely build-out under what was then the zoning (left), and the alternative build-out possible now that an environment-based amendment has been added to the zoning code (this page). These maps are from a comprehensive plan by Jonathan Barnett and Steven Kent Peterson in association with Manuel S. Emanuel Associates, as are Illustrations 39 and 40.

Environmental zoning works best in association with planned unit development ordinances that permit buildings to be clustered in the most buildable areas of the property. Planned unit development in turn works best in association with environmental zoning which prevents excessive densities from being transferred to the portions of the site most suitable for new construction.

Irvington is a maturing community with an already well-defined character and relatively little commercial and industrial land. The environmental amendments to zoning are sufficient to promote sustainable development. In the areas around the Pittsburgh airport, the commercial and industrial zoning in ecologically sensitive areas needs to be remapped in more suitable locations.

In suburban fringe areas with a dispersed pattern of growth, an environmental zoning overlay will disperse development even more, so an additional measure is needed: the growth boundary.

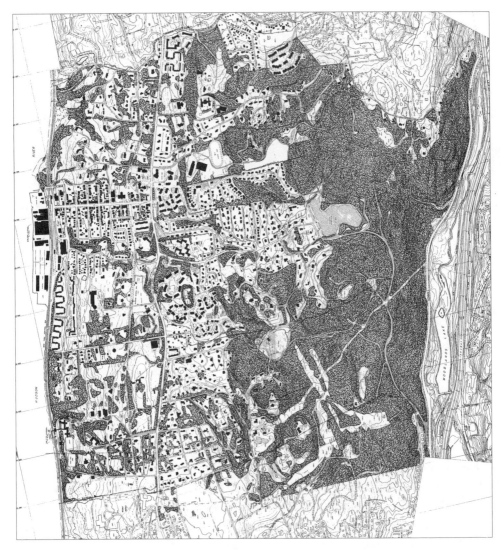

39. A map of Irvington in 1987 showing how much natural area still remained.

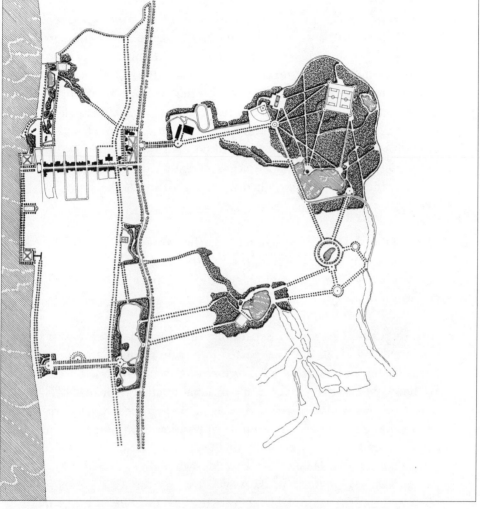

40. *A diagram of Irvington's permanent open space system, which combines village-owned land with natural systems saved by environmental zoning.*

So many farms and woodlands have turned into cities and suburbs that there is often an expectation that rural land is a temporary use. On a national scale, it is absurd to assume that all rural areas will be urbanized, but large amounts of rural land are under pressure from development expectations, far more land than will ever actually be needed. Zoning ordinances establish theoretical development potential, property assessors raise the tax base according to the zoning, and banks lend money to farmers on the value the land might have in the future and not on current use. Even where the zoning is officially rural, there is often an expectation that the regulations can be changed to accommodate a development proposal, or the land is in an unincorporated area where there are few development restrictions.

The result is the familiar disconnected urban growth pattern, which includes not just rapid urbanization at the fringe, but the lack of building in bypassed areas of older cities and in unfinished suburban communities.

Growth boundaries clearly separating land that may one day be urbanized from land that is expected to remain rural are the essential first step in managing all new building in undeveloped areas. Without the boundary there is a continual tendency for urbanization to leapfrog outwards, seeking cheaper land prices, fewer rigorous regulations, and less community opposition. Consider the map [41] prepared by the Greenbelt Alliance of the San Francisco Bay Area, showing that 600,000 acres in the region are at risk of suburban sprawl development in the next 30 years (the dark gray and black areas of the map). Only about a third of this land is likely to be used, although there will probably be some new building in each risk area noted. With modest increases in density, but otherwise conventional development, only about 100,000 acres would be needed, one sixth of the area currently at risk. If there were less abandonment of existing cities, if more new investment went into bypassed parts of already urbanized areas, if new development were in "pedestrian pockets" or other kinds of planned communities compact enough to be served by rapid transit, then even less new land would be needed.

Individual communities like Petaluma, California, and Ramapo,

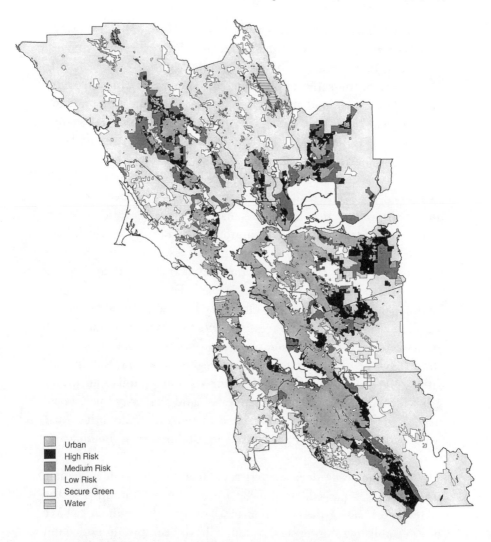

	Urban
	High Risk
	Medium Risk
	Low Risk
	Secure Green
	Water

41. *Map prepared by the San Francisco Bay Area's Greenbelt Alliance showing how much open land is at risk unnecessarily because of poorly drafted development policies.*

New York, have asserted their right to relate development to water resources and utility construction, a principle known as concurrency, and their assertions have been sustained in the courts. Boulder, Colorado, took the implications of concurrency one step further by putting all land above a specific elevation out of bounds for development because of difficulties in pumping water. Many communities use agricultural or very-large-lot zoning to create de facto growth boundaries. While cities and counties can take growth management measures on their own, it is easier to maintain these policies when they are mandated by the state and repeal is not a potential local election issue. It is also easier for localities that are trying to promote growth if all communities in the state are playing by a similar rule book. Land use is a local issue, but the power to regulate land use comes from the state, and as urban regions become larger and larger, the state is needed as ringmaster for local land-use decisions. Ten states currently have growth-management legislation that goes beyond requirements for environmental impact analysis and sets actual standards for development, and most other states have planning agencies. The Oregon state plan requires all cities to estimate their future land needs and establish an urban growth boundary that clearly separates land that may one day be urbanized from land that is expected to remain rural. Cities must work with the surrounding counties to establish these boundaries.

These are not easy decisions. It took from 1973, when Oregon's legislation was passed, until 1986 for all the communities in the state to designate growth boundaries. Now that the boundaries have been established, however, developers have been put on notice not to expect major changes outside the boundaries, and state funds for new highway interchanges, road widenings, urban levels of water and sewer service, and other similar expenditures can be targeted to areas where growth is planned.

Florida's growth-management legislation is based on the principle of concurrency, that is, new development should not take place unless the road, utility, and services infrastructures are already present, or funded so that they will be completed at the same time as development. The locations of future infrastructure and services then establish the areas where growth will be permitted. Under state law, localities are required to prepare new comprehensive plans and rewrite their development regulations to include concurrency. Developments of regional impact—which under a previous Florida law require a special state approval process—must demonstrate that they have the necessary infrastructure and service support before they can be approved.

The process of replanning the state is close to completed, and there has been an official review of planning procedures to suggest improvements.

An unanticipated consequence of concurrency requirements has been a bias toward turning growth away from established urban centers because of predictions of traffic congestion. It comes down to a judgment whether having cars back up in a few downtown blocks for a few minutes each day is an acceptable consequence of concentrating development. Most people would say yes; but if traffic engineering criteria for city streets and close-in highway connectors are the same as the criteria for highways, the answer comes up no.

Another problem with concurrency is its tendency to promote the extension of existing systems, even when the extension takes development into sensitive areas that would better be passed over. That is why the Washington state plan requires local governments to combine provisions similar to Florida's concurrency regulations with growth boundaries like Oregon's.

The public policy implications of using growth boundaries to create compact urban centers in the suburbs were illustrated in the Vision 2020 project sponsored by the Puget Sound Council of Governments. A newspaper supplement was published in May 1990, outlining the development alternatives illustrated by aerial perspectives. One perspective [42] shows the Seattle-Tacoma region as it exists today. It was contrasted with four alternative growth scenarios. The first assumes that local governments continue with their current plans, resulting in the urbanization of 750 additional square miles by 2020. The second alternative postulates a tight urban growth boundary, with development coordinated to keep most new construction within six major centers in the region, thus reducing the estimated urbanization of undeveloped land to 450 square miles. A

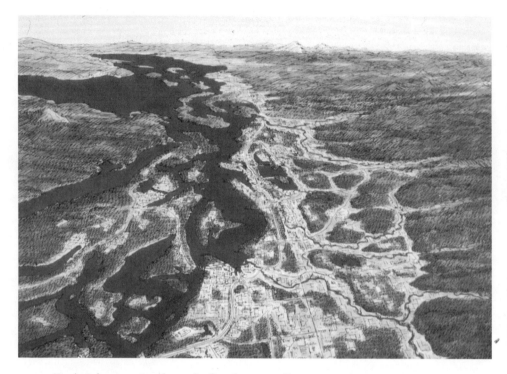

42. *Aerial perspective shows the Seattle metropolitan area as it is at present.*

43. *This perspective shows how urbanization will spread if local governments in the Seattle region keep on with current policies.*

44. *This plan shows how concentrating the majority of development in urban centers will save large areas of the natural landscape and create development patterns suitable for rapid transit. (Drawings in Illustrations 42, 43, 44 prepared for the Vision 2020 Project, Puget Sound Council of Governments, by Hewitt Isley, with assistance by Jack Sidener and Barbara Seymour.)*

third alternative, with a larger number of urban centers distributed over the region, reduces the new land required to 400 square miles. The fourth scenario extrapolates the current trend toward decentralized development [43] without any contravening public policies, producing growth over an estimated 950 square miles of currently rural land.

The last image [44] shows the agreed-upon regional plan, adopted in October 1990, which combines the second and third alternatives

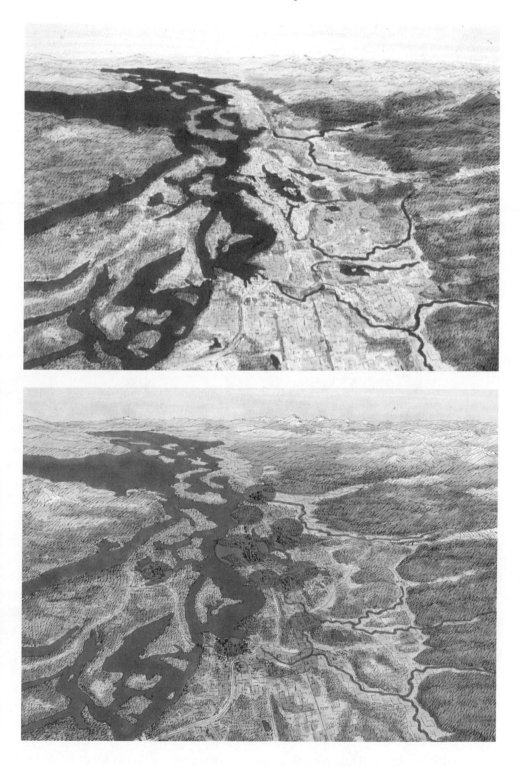

to create a hierarchy of compact centers from Seattle down through five metropolitan cities (Bellevue, Bremerton, Everett, Renton, and Tacoma) to subregional centers, small towns, and suburban development planned as towns. This public policy will be implemented through the design and funding of rapid transit and highway improvements, although selection of the smaller centers has yet to be completed, and those choices involve some very difficult political decisions.

Keying the property tax to the cost of providing services, as is done in the Canadian province of Ontario, is a way of promoting compact development in newly developed areas. The cost of running utilities to houses on small lots set close together is lower than the cost of utility runs to houses on large lots. Another method of promoting compact development in new areas is to draw a tight growth boundary around existing small villages or hamlets, and make sure new development stays within the boundary.

Georgia, where local autonomy is especially strong, based its planning legislation on the ability of the state to withhold economic development funding from local governments whose plans don't meet state standards.

The New Jersey state plan is also based on the state's funding powers. It seeks to establish compatibility among local, county, and state plans, including a consistent set of policies for state agencies. The state is to use its ability to allocate money for highways and infrastructure to encourage the implementation of the plan, particularly to encourage reinvestment in existing centers and reward local governments that regulate new development into compact communities.

The state plan was adopted through a cross-acceptance process of negotiation between the state planning agency and local governments. The preliminary plan, issued in 1989, met with serious opposition, leading to a much-revised interim plan produced in 1991. The initial document appeared to direct most new investment toward existing centers. If that was the original intention, it has been diluted; and specific policies illustrated by drawings have been replaced by generalized goals statements without illustrations.

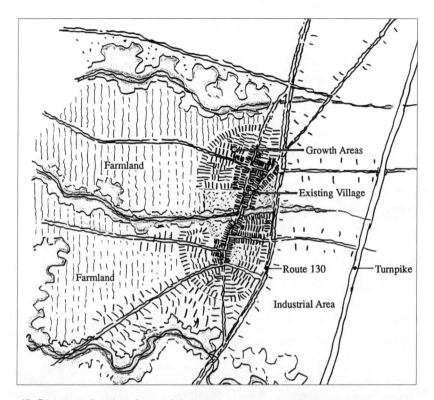

45. *Diagram of projected growth boundaries around the village of Cranbury, New Jersey, prepared by Robert Brown and Robert Geddes of GBQC Architects.*

Nevertheless, the New Jersey state plan says very clearly that in a period of diminished resources government expenditures should be targeted to reinforce appropriate development patterns, although such patterns have yet to be agreed to in detail by local governments and the state.

Hawaii, Maine, Rhode Island, and Vermont also have growth-management legislation; at this writing, California, Connecticut, Maryland, Massachusetts, New York, North Carolina, Pennsylvania, and Virginia are considering some new form of growth management. All these states are feeling the negative effects of rapid urbanization.

Even with growth boundaries and concurrency, there may still be land that should be protected from any development at all, which ultimately means acquisition of the land or its development rights by a government or a conservation trust. In some cases, such as the land around a reservoir, it may be possible to justify land acquisition costs by proof that buying watershed lands and preserving them is more economical than building the water treatment plants that would be necessary if the watershed were developed.

In any case, it is easier to finance such purchases if the land value has not been inflated by overzoning. Nevertheless, money has to be raised from private donors or appropriated from scarce government funds. The federal government acquires or reserves land as national parks and forests; states also have parks and reserves, and have passed bond issues to permit acquisition for environmental purposes. The city of Boulder, Colorado, allocates 0.4 percent of the sales tax for open space acquisition. New York's Hudson River Greenway Act allocates 0.2 percent of a hotel occupancy tax in communities within the area boundaries to fund staff for the Greenway Communities Council and a modest level of property acquisition. The act permits the Council to retain funds from year to year and to accept donations to build up a land-acquisition fund.

The experience in administering growth and change in the New Jersey Pine Barrens is a useful model for balancing the rights of owners against the needs of the state for environmental preservation. A federally designated core of land acquired by government is supported by a land management regime, set up by the state, that covers several counties.

Growth boundaries by themselves do not give any guidance to what happens within their limits. Acceptance of the concurrency principle for infrastructure and transportation does not by itself say much about development. Preserving individual parcels of undeveloped land and local environmental zoning ordinances go only part of the way toward ensuring the integrity of the natural environment. Local governments also need to make their regulations more than a defense against undesirable effects. Regulations should also embody a positive statement about what a community should be.

4

Creating Communities

Zoning ordinances are supposed to embody a comprehensive plan for a community's future. The amount of land an ordinance allocates to different zones is based, in theory, on projections of future population and business growth. In practice, zoning tends to accept the land-use patterns prevailing at the time the ordinance is adopted. Large areas of undeveloped land are usually zoned low-density residential as a way of deferring development decisions. If an entrepreneur wishes to propose an alternative within the low-density residential zone, the change has to be negotiated with the authorities. The practice of zoning commercial corridors and downtowns for many times the development that anyone thinks could actually happen is also a way of avoiding controversial decisions. Within a corridor or a downtown, a big project can be built in many possible locations.

Although such zoning has been written to avoid making definite commitments, it turns out to be the direct cause of today's disconnected and formless growth patterns. If communities wish to take control of their future, they need to make choices about what they wish their community to be.

What is a good community? A basic level of community service is taken for granted in the new city although it is harder to achieve in older urban areas. Communities are expected to be safe and clean, and have modern water, sewer, telephone, and electrical services; buildings should meet code requirements; there should be police and fire protection, postal service, and adequate systems for garbage and rubbish collection and disposal. A threshold issue for many people is the quality of the community's schools: the search for affordable housing in safe neighborhoods with good schools is a powerful motivating force in the migration from the old city to the new.

Defining what constitutes a good community, over and above these threshold criteria, is currently the subject of a lively debate centering around the redefinition of neighborhoods. Two models have been proposed as alternatives to current development practice: the Traditional Neighborhood District as outlined in *Towns and Town-Making Principles* by Andres Duany and Elizabeth Plater-Zyberk and the Transit-Oriented District as described by Peter Calthorpe in *The Next American Metropolis.*

Both assume that walking is the best method for traveling short distances and the necessity for automobiles ought to be diminished. Both use a circle with a quarter-mile radius as the defining element for a neighborhood. The quarter-mile limit to the distance that most people are willing to walk has been validated from experience with shopping centers and transit systems.

The neighborhood unit advocated by Andres Duany and Elizabeth Plater-Zyberk, shown in Illustration 46, has essentially reinvented the diagram of the residential neighborhood published by Clarence Perry as part of the New York Regional Survey and Plan of 1929 [47]. Like Perry, Duany and Plater-Zyberk measure the walking distance from neighborhood institutions situated in the center of their community. Also like Perry, they place neighborhood shopping along the edge, where it can be combined with the shopping related to the next adjacent neighborhood.

Peter Calthorpe's transit-oriented design diagram makes neighborhood shopping and a rapid-transit stop the center of a semicircular district, with radial residential streets, in contrast to the more conventional suburban layout, where dead-end streets branch off arterial roads and shopping is zoned in strips. The other half of the area contained within the quarter-mile-radius circle can be designated for industrial or office uses, unlike the Duany/Plater-Zyberk formulation, which draws a complete circle around the neighborhood on the assumption that homes are somewhat removed from sources of employment.

At Laguna West [48], a planned community in Sacramento County, California, designed by Calthorpe, the commercial center is located on one side of the main arterial road. An axial street leads to the

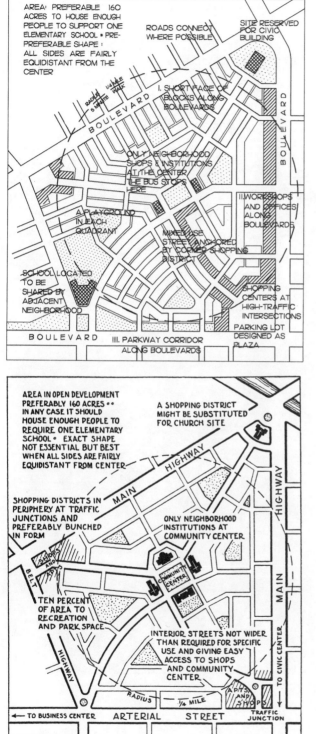

46. *Diagram of a neighborhood prepared by Duany/Plater-Zyberk. Compare with Illustration 47.*

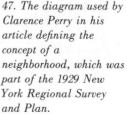

47. *The diagram used by Clarence Perry in his article defining the concept of a neighborhood, which was part of the 1929 New York Regional Survey and Plan.*

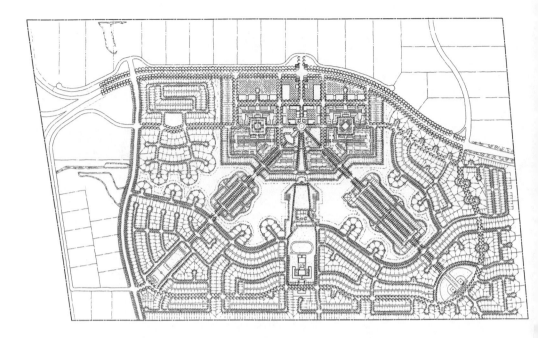

48. *The plan for Laguna West,
a community designed by
Calthorpe Associates. The
public open spaces radiate from
the town center located on the
main highway. The other side
of the highway is an industrial
district.*

49. *This diagram by Peter
Calthorpe shows what he calls
Transit-Oriented Design
Districts located along
rapid-transit routes. Like
Perry's, these districts are
based on a quarter-mile
walking distance, but the
district is a half circle so that
the transit line goes straight to
the center. In the Calthorpe
formulation the other half of
the quarter-mile circle has other
uses and is not part of the
neighborhood, as at Laguna
West.*

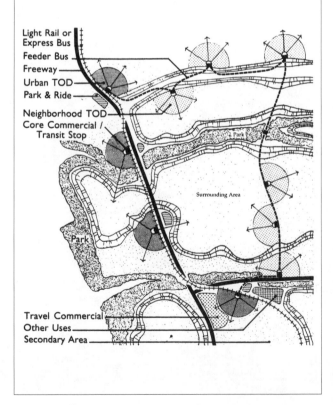

Light Rail or
Express Bus
Feeder Bus
Freeway
Urban TOD
Park & Ride

Neighborhood TOD
Core Commercial /
Transit Stop

Surrounding Area

Park

Park

Travel Commercial
Other Uses
Secondary Area

civic center and then across a lake to a school. Two other radial streets run from the commercial center to residential neighborhoods across the central lake.

Calthorpe has done several regional planning studies showing how transit-oriented communities can be put in place along existing or projected rail routes. Over time, the introduction of these higher development densities could restructure the formless suburbia created during the last generation [49].

Duany and Plater-Zyberk began their career as town planners by designing the village of Seaside, near Santa Rosa Beach on the Florida Panhandle. All of Seaside is only 80 acres, considerably smaller than a single neighborhood with a quarter-mile radius; but under the stewardship of the developer, Robert Davis, Seaside became a laboratory for developing a coherent approach to new suburban and resort development.

The street plan at Seaside is not just a system for automobile access to individual lots. The streets are planned as a network of different experiences, intersected by the main highway that runs through the community. Neighborhood character comes from the shape of the street, the integration of parks and esplanades, and the different destinations visible on the axis of each right of way. The plan encourages people to walk or ride a bicycle from place to place. The town is compact, there are vistas and architectural surprises to keep the journey interesting, and the street environment is designed for pedestrians. The streets in Seaside are narrower and have sharper corners than are permitted by the usual suburban subdivision standards. Speed of auto travel is sacrificed for amenity.

At Seaside, white picket-fences in front of each house define the street in the same way that Raymond Unwin used hedges to separate private and public spaces at Letchworth and Hampstead Garden Suburb. The fences are mandated by the code for Seaside, which replaces local zoning and subdivision controls as part of the planned unit development approved for Seaside under the Walton County zoning ordinance.

A major innovation in the Seaside code is the association of each lot size with a particular building type, and the envelope within which a building type may be constructed is defined in the code. The code specifies conventional bulk controls like height limits and setbacks, but it also includes elements such as mandatory front porches, required roof pitches, and acceptable building materials.

When a designer groups similar lots within a site plan under a code like Seaside's, it is possible to anticipate what the three-dimensional appearance of the buildings will be, in contrast to a conventional site plan, within conventional zoning, where the designer can only determine setbacks and height limits—in other words, what may not be built.

While the association of lots and building types is a genuine innovation, the basic house type at Seaside owes its inspiration to cottages at the pre–World War I resort of De Funiak Springs, about 30 miles to the north. It is easier to describe the intentions of the code by reference to actual buildings rather than a series of abstract formulations. As a result, the early houses at Seaside not only reproduce some of the salient features of cottages to be found at De Funiak Springs; they look like cottages at De Funiak Springs. Duany and Plater-Zyberk continue to assert that the style is not in the code, but the style is what gives Seaside much of its charm. Since traditional buildings were used as the prototype, it should not be displeasing to the planners to have achieved a traditional appearance.

Duany and Plater-Zyberk have now prepared many community plans, mostly for developers building for an upper-income market on large tracts of undeveloped land at the edge of the new city or in resort areas.

Calthorpe's plan for Laguna West accepts typical builder houses. Duany and Plater-Zyberk's plans require a conscious effort, similar to the work of architects during the early part of the twentieth century, to draw inspiration from older towns and villages and revive attractive architectural ideas from other historical periods. Duany and Plater-Zyberk use the phrase "traditional town" to describe the effect they are seeking. This willingness to learn from history has led to a characterization of their work as neotraditional, and the work of their associates and followers as a neotraditional movement. However, they are not designing old-time farm or trading communities, but large, modern suburbs and resorts.

The Duany and Plater-Zyberk plan for Avalon Park covers an area of 9,400 acres east of Orlando, Florida. It is a demonstration of their office's methods applied on a regional scale. Although there is no environmental zoning in effect in the area, Florida's development regulations act like environmental zoning in controlling large, planned projects. The areas of greatest environmental sensitivity at Avalon Park are reserved as open space, and a system of lakes and retention ponds provides drainage and controls water runoff. The natural environment thus becomes the framework for the plan. The plan itself is derived from the mile-square street grid that is laid out over much of Florida, as in many other states.

The aerial photograph [50] shows the main road connections outside the site and the large amount of environmentally sensitive area. The plan [51] creates separate neighborhoods within the natural environment; each neighborhood fits, more-or-less, into a circle with a radius of a quarter of a mile. Four neighborhoods fit together to form a village or town, and there is also a more urban location on the main road with a regional shopping center (also shown in the aerial perspective, Illustration 12).

The main roads connect across the site, and the smaller streets within towns and neighborhoods connect to each other; but Avalon is not like the conventional, right-angle grid plans visible just to the east of the site in Illustration 50. The streets at Avalon, like those at Seaside, are designed to provide a variety of experiences, to incorporate parks and esplanades, to terminate in vistas of the landscape or at important destinations.

The design of Avalon is a modular, repeating system, and it organizes an area far larger than the early-twentieth-century planned communities whose tradition it can be said to continue. If built, Avalon will be two and a half times larger than Letchworth, Ebenezer Howard's prototype garden city, and much of the land area at Letchworth was preserved as a surrounding greenbelt. Avalon would be four times bigger than Clarence Stein and Henry Wright's famous plan for Radburn, New Jersey, and the portion of Radburn

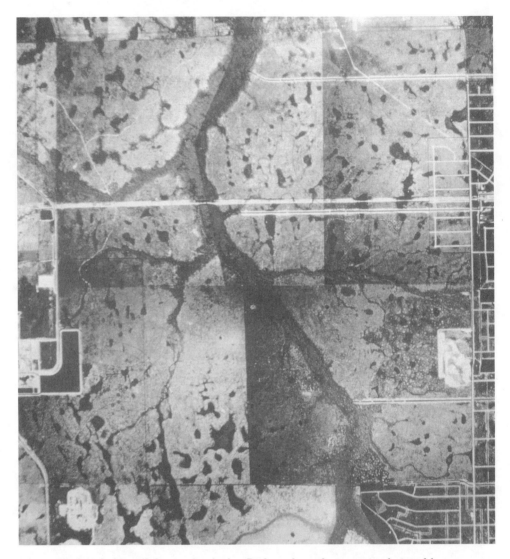

50. *Aerial photo of the site for Avalon Park, a planned community designed by Duany/Plater-Zyberk near Orlando, Florida.*

that was actually built is about as big as Seaside. Neighborhoods at Avalon would be about the same size as such well-known planned suburbs as Forest Hills Gardens, or Mariemont.

If completed as designed, Avalon, by giving primacy to the land-scape, provides a solution to development over large areas that eluded planners of garden suburbs who, ignoring the greenbelt

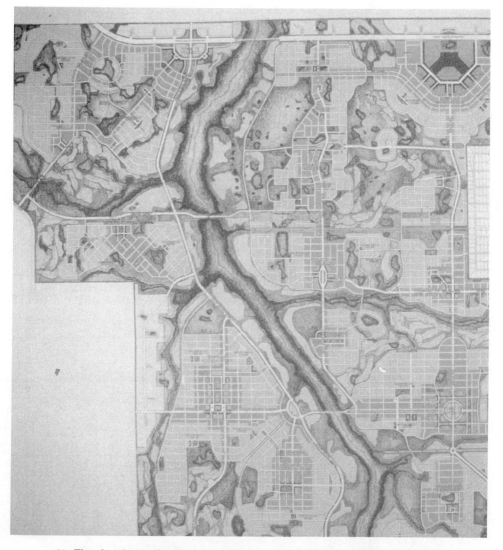

51. *The plan for Avalon Park, showing how the road and neighborhood structure fits into the road system and the sensitive environmental areas visible in Illustration 50.*

tradition, relied on continued extension of the street plan as the controlling design element.

The plan for the 4,500 acres of Daniel Island, in Charleston, South Carolina, is another example of planning at a regional scale where the landscape of tidal wetlands and existing hedgerows has been made the framework for new development [52]. Daniel Island,

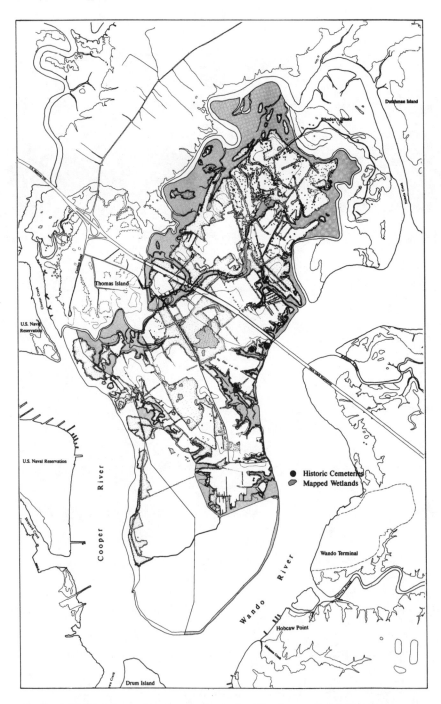

52. Daniel Island, a rural area now annexed to Charleston, South Carolina, where environmentally sensitive waterfront areas and existing hedgerows create a framework for the development plan.

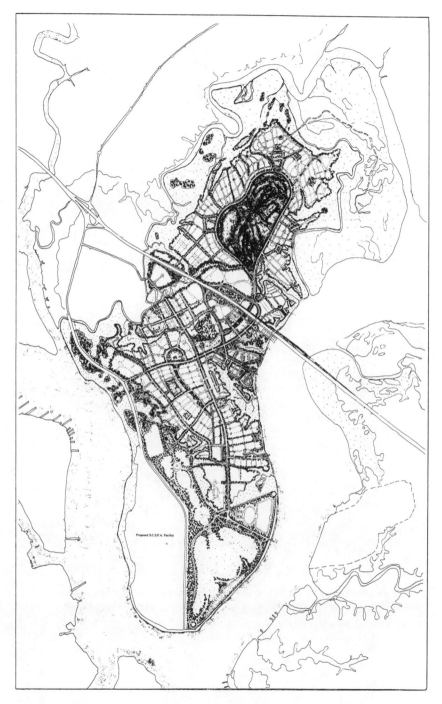

Proposed S.C.S.P.A. Facility

53. *The plan for Daniel Island, by Cooper, Robertson + Partners and Duany/Plater-Zyberk, with Jonathan Barnett and Warren Byrd. The plan is based on neighborhoods, but is not as modular as Avalon Park. The terrain and vegetation, plus the elevated highway that crosses the site, give different parts of the island very specific characteristics.*

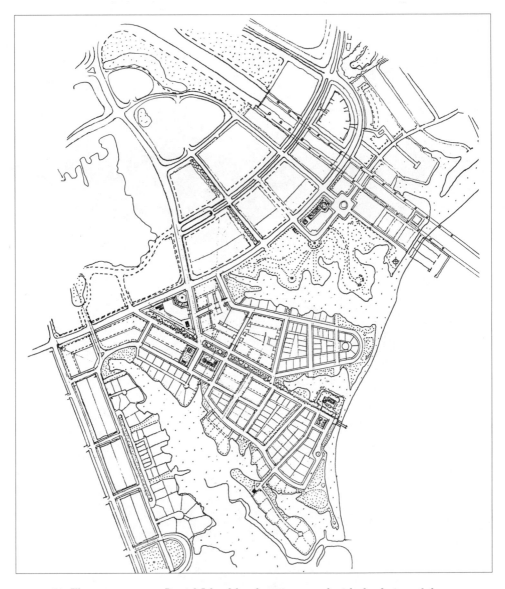

54. The town center at Daniel Island has been integrated with the design of the entrance and exit ramps to the highway, eliminating the conventional cloverleaf. Cars exiting from the highway go directly to the main street of the town, which goes under the highway, raised at this point to cross the Wando River.

where Duany and Plater-Zyberk were part of the planning team, has neighborhoods [53], but they are not as distinctly modular as at Avalon. The town center has been integrated into the design of the on and off ramps of the Mark Clark Expressway, which crosses the site [54].

Both the transit-oriented and traditional neighborhood design concepts have now been written into zoning ordinances. Dade County, Florida, is among the jurisdictions that have adopted a Traditional Neighborhood Development District as an alternative to planned unit development. Neighborhoods must be no smaller than 40 acres and no larger than 200. Larger developments must contain multiple neighborhoods.

Within each neighborhood there must be a mix of residences, shops, workplaces, and civic buildings. There are rules about squares and parks, the street organization and the size and arrangement of blocks, all intended to create the kind of arrangement shown in Illustration 46. Sites for civic buildings are placed in prominent locations. There are rules about sizing streets, and about the character and placement of buildings.

Peter Calthorpe has reinterpreted his experience at Laguna West into Transit-Oriented-District guidelines that have been adopted by Sacramento County.

These kinds of regulations apply primarily to new development; there is a whole task of restoring or creating neighborhoods in already urbanized areas or in fragmented, partially built-up commercial districts. The state of California authorizes local governments to prepare "specific plans" to deal with such situations. These provisions had been in the state code since 1965, attracting little attention until some amendments were made in 1980 that made the specific plan even more effective in repairing faulty zoning and development patterns. Among the 1980 amendments: an exemption from environmental impact statement requirements for any development within the specific plan, as the plan itself must have an impact statement.

A specific plan is like a planned unit development in that an individ-

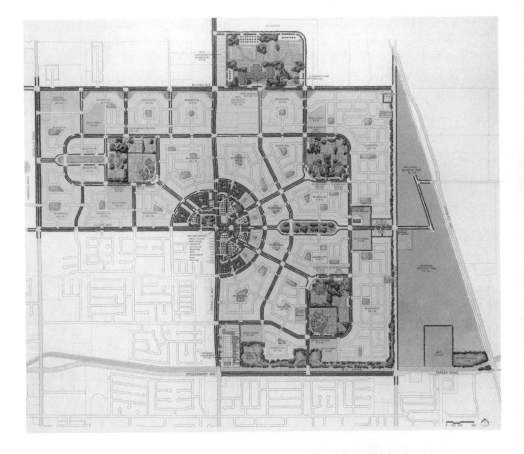

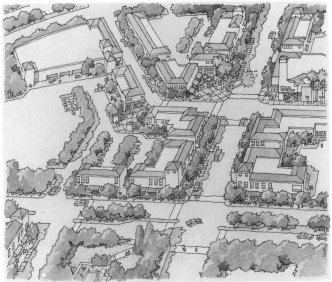

55. The specific plan by the ROMA Design Group for 1,784 acres being annexed by Modesto, California. Instead of continuing conventional grid development, the plan creates a town center, neighborhood centers, and smaller individual communities.

56. Detail of the regional shopping and office center.

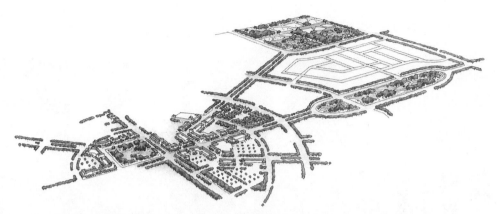

57. *Part of the public open space system in the ROMA plan with greenways leading from the center to the neighborhoods.*

ual design can become the zoning. It differs from planned unit development because it can be prepared on a community's initiative, it can cover any number of separate ownerships, and the preparation of a specific plan, like a zoning ordinance, does not require the consent of the owners involved. Specific plans also resemble urban renewal plans, but there is no need to make findings of blight or deterioration, nor must government acquire any of the property. A local authority that has designated an area for a specific plan can assess the property owners within the designated area for the costs of preparing the plan.

This powerful planning mechanism is not as controversial as might be expected because it also provides big benefits for property owners. Instead of playing zoning like a game with winners and losers, property owners can pool their advantages and attract development that none could have hoped for individually.

A specific plan by ROMA Design Group for an area being annexed by Modesto, California, covers 1,784 acres already divided among 168 separate owners. The site of the specific plan is at the edge of an area of conventional subdivisions. Much of the land is currently agricultural, but there has already been some residential building on big parcels, and several churches have been constructed recently. The plan shows the new development pattern to be created, and the way it fits into and completes the existing street system [55].

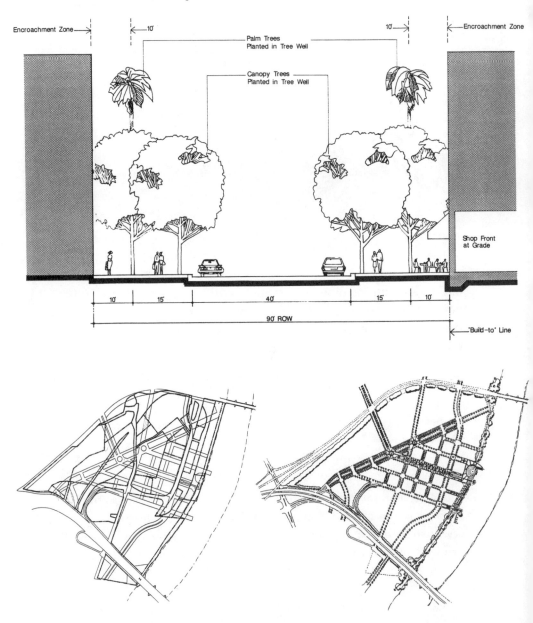

58. *Street section from the downtown Anaheim specific plan by Sedway Cooke Associates. This plan can produce results comparable to urban renewal, but without the need for the municipality to condemn and assemble individual properties.*

59, 60. *The existing property boundaries within the West Sacramento Triangle specific plan (59), compared to the street plan (60) prepared by the Zimmer, Gunsul, Frasca Partnership with Sasaki Associates.*

Instead of more and more conventional subdivisions and a strip commercial street, the plan creates a village center, shown in detail in Illustration 56, connected to the surrounding neighborhoods by radial avenues [57]. The village has enough retail space to function as a regional shopping center, as well as civic places and buildings, multifamily housing, and senior housing. The plan creates three large neighborhood districts around the center. These neighborhoods are larger than the Duany/Plater-Zyberk model, about 500 acres each, but they are divided into subneighborhoods, most of which are from 30 to 50 acres. Each large neighborhood is designed around a central school and park area, and the smaller subneighborhoods also have their own park system. On the east side of the site, near the railway, land has been reserved for industry and a business park. The difference between relying on conventional zoning and subdivision and planning new development as a community is clear.

The same principles can be used to redevelop an existing area, as shown in the specific plan for downtown Anaheim by Sedway Cooke Associates. Here the objective is to create a series of new uses along two business streets that are to be rebuilt as esplanades. The plan sets architectural standards for buildings and their relation to the streets, as shown in the street section [58], much as in an urban renewal plan, but without the need to declare the area blighted. Communities along metropolitan San Francisco's Bay Area Rapid Transit line have used specific plans to shape development around stations. Another example: West Sacramento is using a specific plan prepared by the Zimmer, Gunsul, Frasca partnership with Sasaki Associates to make changes along the waterfront. Note the comparison of the existing property boundaries [59] with the new street plan [60]. Without a specific plan there would be little chance of such a complex property pattern being redeveloped in such a comprehensive way.

Specific plans, Traditional Neighborhood District Ordinances, Transit-Oriented District design guidelines, the kinds of development regulations developed for Avalon or Daniel Island, all provide precedents for affirmative zoning and subdivision that embody a vision of the community's future.

Part II
Restoring the Old City

5

How the Metropolis
Split Apart

T he metropolitan area of the 1950s is still in the back of many
people's minds as the natural condition of cities. It is hard
to accept that it belongs to an ever more distant historical
period. The city in 1950 still preserved the pattern of a central
downtown with office buildings, theaters, and department stores,
plus compact urban neighborhoods and a fringe of leafy residential
suburbs. This pattern had been in place for two generations, and
was connected to an evolutionary process that had been going on for
more than a century. By 1950 the automobile had already set city
development free from streetcar corridors and the relatively small
radius around suburban railway stations. In fact, this enlargement
of urbanized areas had become well established by the 1930s, but
the Great Depression and World War II slowed down the pace of
urban growth.

During the 1950s the form of the modern city had come to seem
permanent, assumed to be a known quantity by social scientists,
city planners, and just about everyone else. It was true that many
people now commuted by automobile instead of train or streetcar,
and there were a few branches of downtown department stores on
suburban main streets, but downtown was still the center for work,
entertainment, and shopping, and most industry was still grouped
along the railways. There was a new airport, usually near downtown,
but the train and the car remained the dominant means of intercity
travel.

One significant change and a portent of changes to come: by the
early 1950s most of the old rich, except in a few large cities (or in
very old-school places like Charleston, South Carolina), had abandoned the traditionally fashionable urban neighborhoods for the
most socially prestigious suburbs, leaving the old city mansions to

be replaced by offices or apartments, converted to institutional uses, or left to deteriorate into inexpensive lodgings.

The strategy of withdrawal by the rich from the vicinity of those less fortunate is the most fundamental shaping force in the development of the modern metropolis. Before the modern era, withdrawal from the close confines of the city was difficult, because everyone needed the walls for protection. The suburbs outside were originally the shantytowns of the poor and the location for tanneries, slaughter-houses, and other unwanted activities. As soon as people of means no longer felt they had to live behind fortifications, however, they sought escape from the crowded and noisome city.

London, protected by England's island location, began to grow outside its walls long before the cities of continental Europe. As early as the 1500s, the Strand, the street leading westward from the walled City of London toward Westminster, was lined with estates and religious institutions. In the seventeenth and eighteenth centu-ries these large land holdings were subdivided to form elegant streets and town squares, the city residences of the aristocracy. Commerce followed the carriage trade westward, so that by the end of the eighteenth century Covent Garden and other areas nearest to the old City of London had become extensions of the commercial center. Covent Garden, the square designed by Inigo Jones in the 1630s and the prototype for much later residential development, turned into a market district, as the rich picked up their possessions and moved farther west.

The creation of a preferred urban residential district, its invasion by commerce, and the establishment of new preferred neighborhoods farther west of the original center is a repeating pattern in the growth of London. Because so much of the industrial revolution began in England, London is really the first modern metropolis, and its growth patterns prefigure the development of all modern metro-politan areas.

The first effects of the industrial revolution on London came from a great increase in trade, leading to the growth of the docklands down the Thames to the east of the City, and the movement of the newly rich to the rapidly growing fashionable districts of London's

West End. In the early stages of industrialization, textile mills and other industries were located far from London in places close to water power or other natural resources.

The railroad and the steam-powered factory brought industry into London beginning in the 1830s, surrounding the original city with an iron ring of noise, pollution, and squalor—except to the west, where property values were too high for industrial development. Industrialization thus sharpened the separation between the poor and the comfortable classes and ensured that those merchants and professionals who had continued to live in the city center would move to the western districts.

Escape to more rural suburbs also began early in London. In the eighteenth century, London merchants—who, unlike the aristocrats, had no country estates—began purchasing land in villages near London to build weekend houses. By 1800 some merchants were living in villa districts within commuting distance of their businesses, going into the city every weekday by carriage. Robert Fishman, an urban historian, considers villages like Clapham, five miles south of London Bridge, the prototype of the modern suburb, what Fishman calls a "bourgeois utopia." Not only were its leading residents commuters, but they were evangelical Christians who had deliberately moved their families out of the bustling and immoral city. The concept of the wife's role as the guardian of a safe haven in the country and the husband as the commuter to the dangerous world of commerce was thus implicit in the suburb from the beginning. But, if Clapham is the ancestor of the modern suburb, the line of descent is complicated. As early suburbs on the less fashionable sides of London were overrun by industry, the rich merchant families moved to join the aristocrats. Soames Forsyte, the character drawn by John Galsworthy as the prototypical upper-middle-class man of property, grew up in London's urbane West End. By the time of the *Forsyte Saga*, the 1880s through the 1920s, Clapham was best known for its railway junction.

Most cities in the United States were founded, like preindustrial cities everywhere, when freight was moved primarily by water. The best city locations were at the confluence of two rivers, where a river meets one of the great lakes, or at a harbor where a river meets the ocean. The first map in a sequence illustrating the growth of a generic North American city shows a settlement at the confluence of two rivers [61]. Some later cities, like Atlanta, grew up at railway terminals, but most cities that owed their growth primarily to railroads, like Seattle or Dallas, were originally settlements located on waterways. As in England, early factories like those in Lowell, Massachusetts, and Paterson, New Jersey, were built at waterfalls, which almost by definition were far away from the navigable routes where established cities were located. An early industrial location is shown upstream from the city in Illustration 61.

Like their counterparts in London, the rich in U.S. cities began moving to fashionable residential districts away from the poor, and the noise and congestion of the business centers. By the early nineteenth century Beacon Hill in Boston, Washington Square in New York, and the area around the Monument in Baltimore were fashionable districts. Such neighborhoods established a preferred, or right, side of the city which later became the point of origin for a mansion street: Beacon Street in Boston, Fifth Avenue in New York, Charles Street in Baltimore, St. Charles Avenue in New Orleans, Euclid Avenue in Cleveland, Lindell Boulevard in St. Louis, California Street in San Francisco. The beginnings of a mansion street show up on the second map of our generic North American City [62].

In the older, denser cities such as Boston, New York, and Baltimore, the mansion street, which included the most fashionable clubs and places of worship, was part of an elegant urban district of attached houses, like the West End of London. In smaller cities like New Orleans or Cleveland the mansions were almost all separate villas on landscaped plots, like houses in Clapham or such early U.S. suburbs as Llewellyn Park, New Jersey, or Riverside, an early railway suburb of Chicago. The mansion street generally led to a park with an art museum in it and to the city's most socially prestigious college or university.

By the 1880s most American cities were part of a national railway network, had large industrial districts along the railway tracks, and often a subsidiary city, almost purely industrial, across the river or harbor from the original settlement, as shown in the next stage of

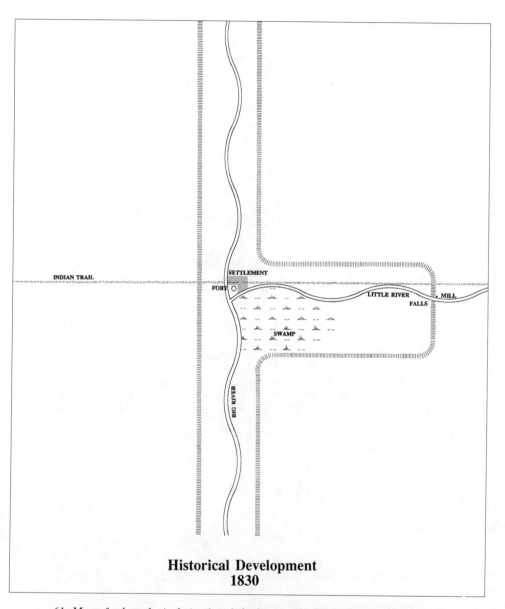

INDIAN TRAIL

SETTLEMENT

FORT

LITTLE RIVER

FALLS

MILL

SWAMP

BIG RIVER

**Historical Development
1830**

61. *Map of a hypothetical city founded when settlers build a fort at the confluence of the Little and Big rivers, the same location that Native Americans had selected earlier as a village or campsite. There is a separate industrial development at the falls of the Little River to the west.*

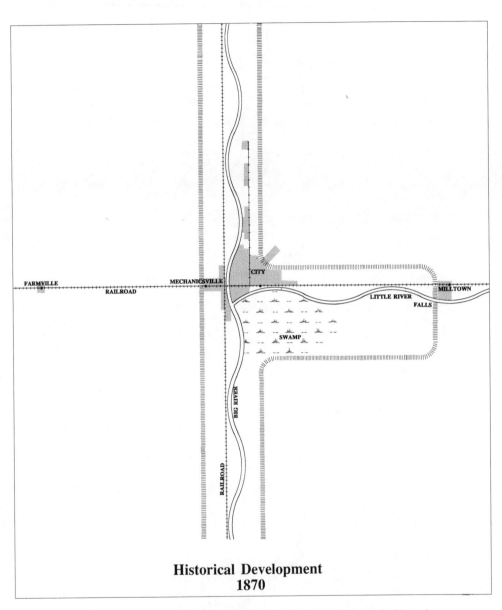

**Historical Development
1870**

62. The railroads arrive by the 1860s, following the river valleys and old trails, and the city begins to expand. A sibling city is founded across the Big River. The rich have begun moving up to the hills northeast of the city center.

development of the hypothetical city mapped in Illustration 62. Actual examples include Camden, New Jersey, across the Delaware River from Philadelphia, or East St. Louis, Illinois.

The railroad and the streetcar extended the geographic area of the city and led to intensified urban development downtown, the most famous instances of this trend being the skyscrapers within the Chicago Loop and near the subway stations in lower Manhattan. By 1914 most cities had some tall office buildings in their downtown financial districts, plus a whole series of other distinct areas: the city government and courts were likely to be downtown near the financial district, further uptown—that is in the direction of the mansion street—there would be a theater district, a concentration of department stores, and a midtown area of hotels, clubs, fashionable shops, and apartments. There would also be a warehouse and factory district near the docks and railway, a sin district, a skid row, and various downtown low-income neighborhoods. Illustrations 73 and 74 show these typical downtown districts.

Innovations in transportation created a new kind of geographic segregation. The poor continued to live within walking distance of mills and factories, and the rich in their mansion districts. The lower middle classes took street railways from new residential neighborhoods on the expanding edge of the city, and the upper middle class took trains from suburban areas that had grown up around railway stations, such as the Main Line suburbs of Philadelphia. These railroad suburbs were also places where the rich had their summer estates [63].

As the American population grew through successive waves of immigration, older neighborhoods developed distinctive ethnic characters. Suburbs also developed individual social profiles, often reinforced by deed restrictions: Oak Park, on the western side of Chicago, became truly a bourgeois utopia; Lake Forest, on the more fashionable North Shore, became a great deal more pretentious. Like other suburbs on the fashionable side of American cities, it became a place to recreate the grand houses of the English landed gentry and the atmosphere of an established, hierarchical social order.

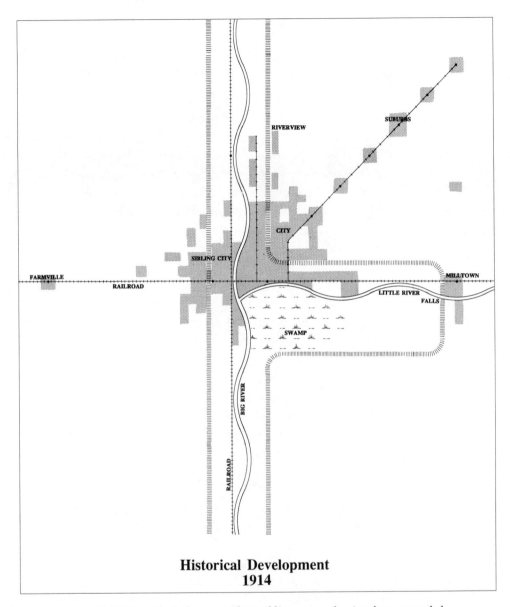

Historical Development
1914

63. By World War I both the city and its sibling across the river have expanded along streetcar lines. A railroad leads to a string of fashionable suburbs to the northeast, and metropolitan growth has reached the factory town up at the falls of the Little River.

The pattern of city development that persisted throughout the 1950s [64] has now given way to the modern, fractured metropolis [65]. The old social geography, where one sector of the city, selected by the rich, was the residential location of choice for the executive and professional classes, has become the new business geography, the latest extension of the principle seen long ago at Covent Garden that commerce follows the carriage trade.

The older parts of the city are left with a physical fabric that was created for economic and social conditions that no longer exist.

Downtown has lost its monopoly position as the regional center, and is now just one of a chain of business districts leading to the rapidly urbanizing fashionable suburbs, the new executive office parks, and the substantial cluster of office buildings at the new international airport. Many people consider it a point of honor to be able to say that they never go downtown at all: they work, shop, and find entertainment or cultural events without leaving what used to be called suburbia [66].

The new metropolitan center is likely to be along the portion of the ring road or bypass highway located midway between the city's country-club district and the older upper-income suburbs. This highway has become the main street for new development on the fashionable side of the city.

Downtown may still have a significant concentration of shops and department stores and new retail malls on the suburban model; but all the best stores can also be found in shopping centers where the old mansion street meets the ring road, or at the junction of the ring and the radial highways that flank the fashionable sector. There are more modest retail malls, which also duplicate shopping opportunities in the city center and the older suburban downtowns, serving the rest of the metropolitan area. Newer, larger malls with better highway access have now started driving out of business the earlier shopping centers in older, congested areas, and established stores are becoming vulnerable to competition from new kinds of discount retailing, catalogue sales, and televised shopping. The commercial patterns shown in Illustration 66 could be subject to yet another generation of urban dislocation.

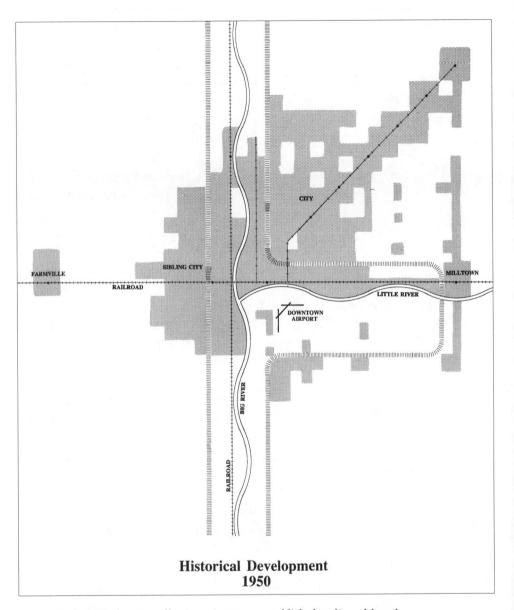

Historical Development
1950

64. In 1950 the city still preserves patterns established earlier, although automobile-supported development has filled in and expanded the corridors along streetcar lines and railroads. There is now an airport on the low-lying land just south of the city center.

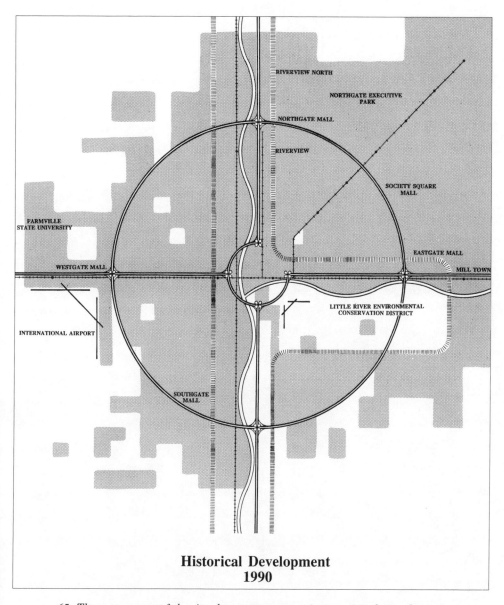

RIVERVIEW NORTH

NORTHGATE EXECUTIVE
PARK

NORTHGATE MALL

RIVERVIEW

SOCIETY SQUARE
MALL

FARMVILLE
STATE UNIVERSITY

EASTGATE MALL

WESTGATE MALL

MILL TOWN

INTERNATIONAL AIRPORT

LITTLE RIVER ENVIRONMENTAL
CONSERVATION DISTRICT

SOUTHGATE
MALL

**Historical Development
1990**

65. *The current map of the city shows an enormous increase in urbanized area,
with a new rifle-sight pattern superimposed by the interstate highways and
circular bypass road. There is a new, larger airport west of the city.*

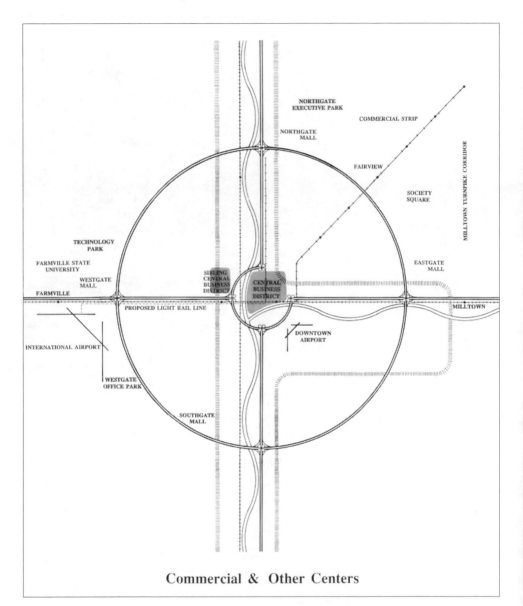

Commercial & Other Centers

66. The old urban downtown and the downtown of the sibling city remain, as do the old neighborhood and suburban centers, but they are in competition with new suburban shopping centers built at the point where the east-west and north-south highways intersect the ring road. There is a new office and industrial complex out by the airport west of the city, and important office parks and specialty retail centers have appeared in the fashionable northeast quadrant of the city.

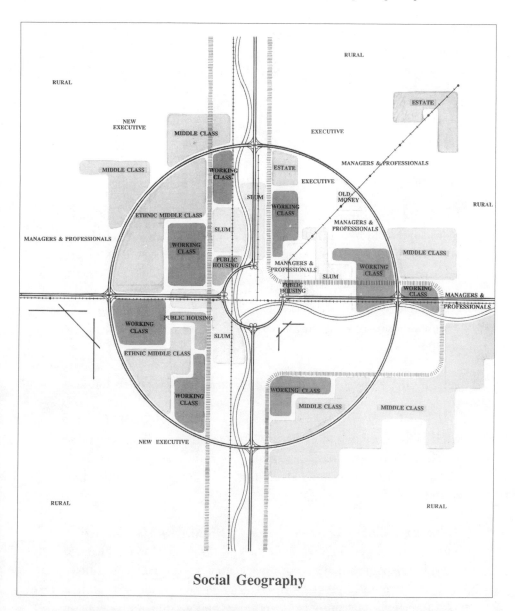

Social Geography

67. *Comparison of the commercial centers with the metropolitan area's social geography shows that commerce still follows the geographic patterns set by the carriage trade, as most of the city's affluent people live in the northeast quadrant. The exception to the prevailing affluence in the northeast is the old factory town at the falls, which has been absorbed into the larger urban development pattern. However, the ring road seems to free people from old real estate patterns, and new upper-income development can also be found on the unfashionable western side of the city, near the airport.*

A sequence of maps showing the development of Kansas City provides a comparison with the generic city map sequence. The original settlement began at the confluence of the Missouri and Kansas rivers. Two nearby towns, Independence and Westport, the gateway to the Santa Fe trail, already existed [68].

By the late nineteenth century the railroads had made Kansas City, Missouri, an important center, and Kansas City, Kansas, had developed as a sibling city across the Kansas River [69].

By World War I the city had grown substantially, the new development supported by a streetcar system that opened up new neighborhoods and residential suburbs. Kansas City also created an elaborate park and boulevard system, one of the most successful examples of the City Beautiful movement. The direction of the mansion street was southward from the city center and the J. C. Nichols company had established the country club district at the southern edge of the city.

In 1950 the Kansas City metropolitan area had expanded but still centered on the original downtown and the Country Club Plaza, now developed as an uptown shopping and apartment house district. The fashionable residential neighborhoods had extended southwest from the plaza and across the state line to Mission Hills in Kansas. The map shows an airport across the river just north of downtown.

Today's map shows a vast expansion of urbanized area supported by a new highway system. Overland Park, Kansas, southwest of Kansas City, has become a major new office center. People can commute to it easily from the affluent southwestern neighborhoods and suburbs of Kansas City or from new townhouses and garden apartments on the urban fringe, and far less easily from the poorer districts in the northeast part of the old city. With the completion of the outer highway ring road, it is possible to drive directly north to the new Kansas City International Airport—which has replaced the old downtown airport—without going through Kansas City at all.

Kansas City, like many another urban area, had a wave of new downtown office development in the 1980s, and a small boom in office space at the midtown Crown Center. The Country Club Plaza has become more of a metropolitan center than downtown, the location for the best shops. There has been some new office development at the Plaza, but the majority of new office space has been built in Overland Park or north of the city, near the airport.

Some of the urban mansion districts of the old rich have been converted to offices or apartments that house a professional-class population, and the city has helped finance the rejuvenation of the Quality Hill neighborhood near downtown. The comeback of old high-income areas in many cities does not represent a general return of rich and influential people to the city center. Today the older country-club districts come closest to having the status of the only socially acceptable place to live—very much the case in Kansas City—but rich people in most metropolitan areas now have many choices and may commute from distant, resortlike locations or live in urban and suburban apartment buildings or even in an old urban mansion.

Industrial pollution has always been a major reason for people to move out of cities; but now industry itself is moving out. In Kansas City the stockyards are almost deserted, and much other downtown industry has been replaced by outlying industrial parks where land is cheap and readily available. As in other cities, factory workers now commute outward from city neighborhoods, or from new subdivisions, apartment colonies and mobile home parks on the urban fringe.

Warehouses have followed factories to fringe locations near highway interchanges. In the Kansas City metropolitan area there are substantial warehouse districts along highways in the southwest quadrant. Goods no longer travel from larger center to smaller center by train, to be broken down into smaller lots for local delivery. Instead, most freight moves directly from factories to distribution warehouses to destinations in patterns that follow highways and railroads but ignore the old hierarchy of cities—which are now just destinations like every other place in the new system. The sight of a trailer truck as big as a railway freight car parked in front of the local supermarket is a small indication of a major revolution in transportation.

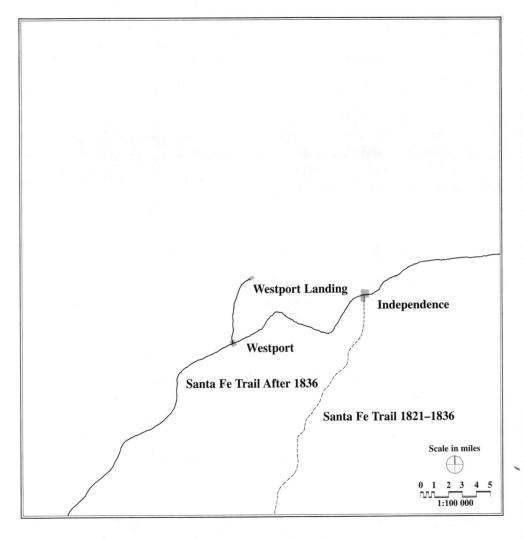

Historical Development
1840

68. When Kansas City began as a settlement at the confluence of the Missouri and Kansas rivers, Independence and Westport, the gateway to the Santa Fe Trail, already existed.

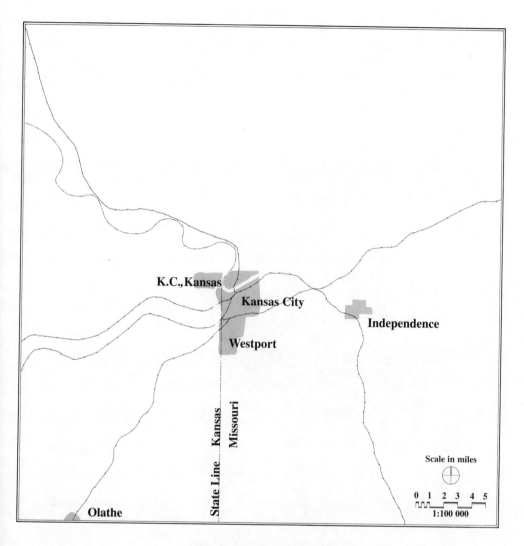

K.C.,Kansas

Kansas City

Independence

Westport

State Line   Kansas
Missouri

Scale in miles

0 1 2 3 4 5

1:100 000

Olathe

Historical Development
1880

69. By the late nineteenth century the railroads had made Kansas City, Missouri, an important center, and Kansas City, Kansas, had developed as a sibling city.

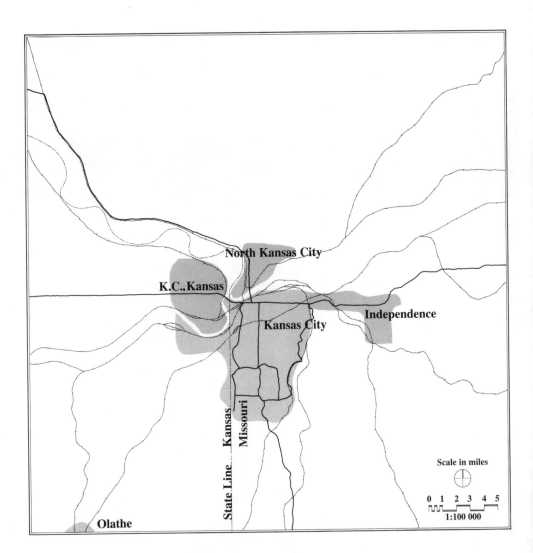

Historical Development
1919

70. By World War I, the city had grown substantially. Streetcars had helped residential neighborhoods develop, notably the Country Club district south of the city center.

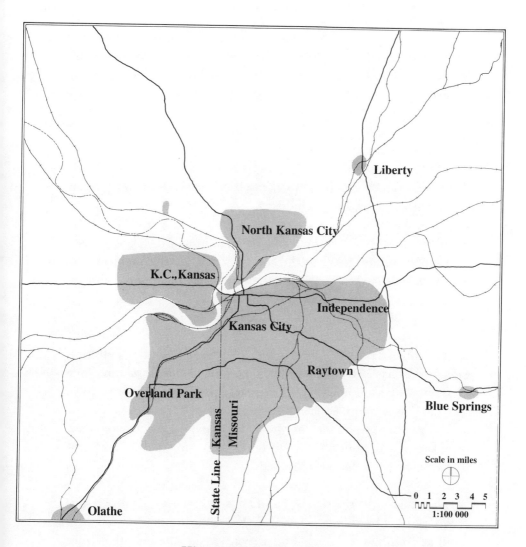

Historical Development
1950

71. In 1950 the Kansas City metropolitan area had expanded but was still centered around downtown and the shopping in the Country Club district, with the fashionable residential districts mostly in the southwest quadrant. There is now an airport on low-lying land north of the city center.

In all older cities the migration of industry has pulled away many of the lower rungs of the economic ladder. Urban neighborhoods, particularly areas of tenements, are partly deserted and half destroyed; walk-to-work districts near now-disused factories are in transition, with older families hanging on and new immigrants moving in. Other neighborhoods have had a complete population change in the last generation, having gone from white to black, or from one ethnic or language group to another.

No one wants to go back to the settlement patterns and social hierarchies of feudal or preindustrial society, or even to the United States of the 1920s and 30s, when racial, religious, and sex discrimination were taken for granted and when, in Franklin Delano Roosevelt's phrase, one third of the nation was ill-housed, ill-clad and ill-nourished. However, the new metropolitan geography, with its fragmentation of traditional communities and the migration of jobs away from older urban centers, is a major cause not only of environmental stress and traffic gridlock but of unemployment, alienation, and the breakdown of law and order. The evolution of the metropolitan region has left most low-income people concentrated in older deteriorating neighborhoods of cities and towns, while jobs and the tax base to support education and social services have migrated elsewhere. Separating the poor from access to jobs and leaving them in places where both public and private investment is being withdrawn is a recipe for social tragedy.

At the same time, the removal of dirty smokestack industries from cities is an extraordinary development opportunity. Not only are land and buildings available for new uses, but the pollution from these industries was the reason why so many people migrated to more pleasant suburban areas as soon as they could afford to do so. The lesson from history is that no urban area will prosper unless it attracts the people who can choose to live wherever they wish.

The last time the U.S. made a major commitment to solving urban problems was in the mid-1960s, but these Great Society programs, whatever their merits might have been, were never funded above an experimental level. The money was spent instead on the Vietnam war, a huge economic commitment over and above the high national defense costs of the Cold War era. In addition, the burden

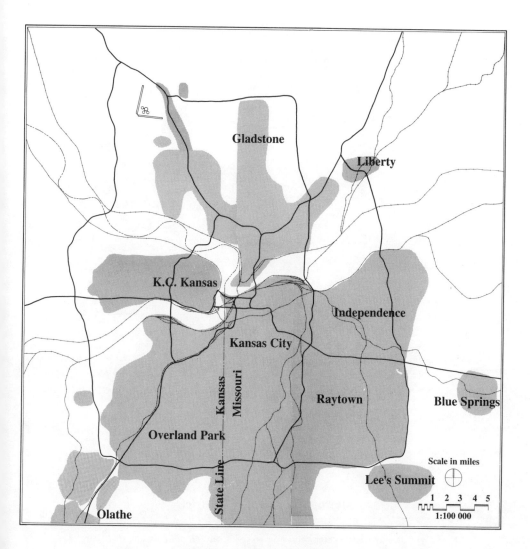

Historical Development
1989

72. Today the highway system and peripheral roads have imposed a different pattern, connecting Overland Park, the new urban center in the southwest, to the commercial development at the new airport to the far northwest of the city. The real commercial center of the city has shifted southward, with the shops in the Country Club district, once occupied by local service businesses, becoming the region's leading retail location.

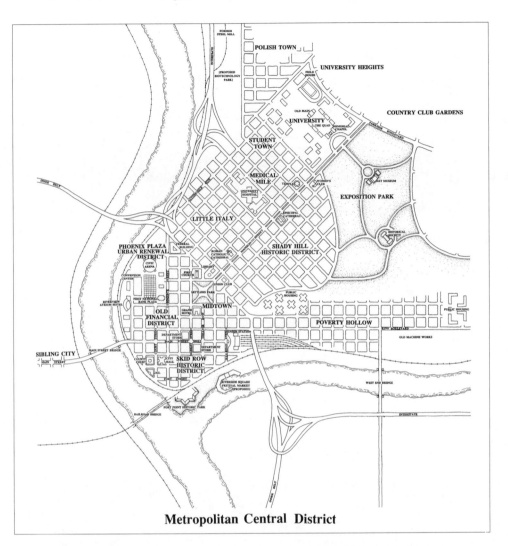

FORMER STEEL MILL

POLISH TOWN

UNIVERSITY HEIGHTS

INTERSTATE

(PROPOSED BIOTECHNOLOGY PARK)

FIELD HOUSE

OLD MAIN

UNIVERSITY

THE QUAD

MEMORIAL CHAPEL

COUNTRY CLUB GARDENS

PARK BOULEVARD

STUDENT TOWN

INNER BELT

MEDICAL MILE

UNIVERSITY HOSPITAL

TEMPLE

WOMEN'S CLUB

ART MUSEUM

EXPOSITION PARK

LITTLE ITALY

EPISCOPAL CATHEDRAL

HISTORICAL SOCIETY

PHOENIX PLAZA URBAN RENEWAL DISTRICT

FEDERAL BUILDING

ROMAN CATHOLIC CATHEDRAL

LIBRARY

SHADY HILL HISTORIC DISTRICT

CIVIC ARENA

CONVENTION CENTER

FIRST CHURCH

RIVERVIEW ATRIUM HOTEL

FIRST NATIONAL BANK PLAZA

SETTLERS PARK

UNION CLUB

PUBLIC HOUSING

GRAND HOTEL

MIDTOWN

PUBLIC HOUSING

OLD FINANCIAL DISTRICT

POVERTY HOLLOW

KING BOULEVARD

DEPARTMENT STORE

DEPARTMENT STORE

UNION STATION

OLD MACHINE WORKS

SIBLING CITY

MAIN STREET BRIDGE

COUNTY COURT

CITY HALL

SKID ROW HISTORIC DISTRICT

MAIN STREET

WEST END BRIDGE

RIVERSIDE SQUARE FESTIVAL MARKET (PROPOSED)

FORT POINT HISTORIC PARK

RAILROAD BRIDGE

INTERSTATE

INNER BELT

Metropolitan Central District

73. *The hypothetical city center shown in more detail. The old financial district is at the original settlement location. An adjacent warehouse district has become an urban renewal area, with a convention center, atrium hotel, the riverfront arena, and the headquarters of the leading local bank. The government district is adjacent to the financial district. Near the remains of the old fort is a new festival marketplace now proposed as a location for riverboat gambling. Farther uptown is the old department store district, now fronting on a landscaped transit way, and the location of old theaters, one of which has now become a cultural center. In the midtown area, surrounding the park named in honor of early settlers, can be found the old fashionable hotel (now housing for senior citizens), the public library, and the most prestigious club. The old mansion street goes up the hill from midtown, heading for the university and the Centennial Park, created during the City Beautiful movement at the beginning of the twentieth*

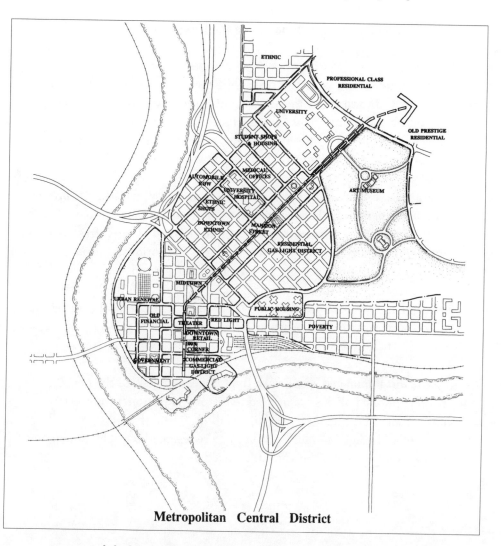

Metropolitan Central District

century and the location for the art museum and the historical society. The
Episcopal and Roman Catholic cathedrals and a major synagogue are all on the
mansion street, which is now mostly office buildings and apartment houses. The
old mansions near the hospital are all doctors' offices, or student housing for the
university, but there is also a historic district, where big old houses have been
restored as apartments or individual homes. Down the hill from the historic
neighborhood, along the railway tracks, is poverty hollow, site of the city's first
housing project and still its most deteriorated area. Along the river to the north
are disused factories, now designated the site for a biotechnology park.

74. The same hypothetical, but typical, downtown mapped as a series of districts
(above).

of the war fell disproportionately on the least well-off sectors of our society.

In the absence of a constructive public policy for improving urban areas, withdrawal from the cities continues and may even be accelerating. Stopping the decline of older cities requires new initiatives, not palliatives whose best hope would be to slow down economic and social changes that are by now irreversible.

These new initiatives will require substantial new investment, but the investment, whether private or public, can be made to pay off. A tremendous inventory of valuable buildings and urban infrastructure, plus established businesses, cultural institutions, and neighborhood traditions, is tied up in old metropolitan centers, and other, smaller old cities. Attracting new investment to the bypassed areas of the older city is also the other side of the coin of policies to restrict growth at the urban fringe. One policy will not work without the other.

In the most damaged areas, with their concentrations of the poorest people, public policies are needed to restore education, promote law and order, and encourage family stability. But the most critical issue of all is that older cities need to be redesigned so their tremendous economic potential can be realized.

6

The Entrepreneurial Center

An urban downtown these days is a high-risk entrepreneurial business, and cities are in it whether they like it or not. Imagine that you are a mayor, contemplating your city's financial future during the annual budget review. The city's best sources of revenue are all tied to the downtown business district. Downtown has the prime concentration of real estate values to support the property tax, although lately, because of vacant office space and slower retail trade, assessments on many properties have had to be reduced. Even in bad times, however, downtown is still a major generator of the payroll, sales, and hotel-room taxes. Every year the cost of providing social services goes up, and tax rates have been raised to the point where they are making the city uncompetitive. There is some assistance from the state and federal governments, but no one is talking about big increases in outside aid. The logical conclusion is a policy of preserving downtown business and assisting its future growth, to improve the revenue base for the whole city.

Some years ago the city invested in a convention and exhibition center. It is not exactly a money-maker, and the annual debt service is a major budgetary hit, but it improves tax receipts because it has raised downtown hotel occupancy, and downtown retailers also see improved business when conventions come to town. Now, however, the managers of the convention center advise that they need to expand to stay competitive. They think there may be state funds available for the expansion, but a larger center will also require the support of another hotel.

The redevelopment authority has a potential deal with a hotel developer, but the investors are looking for 10 years of property tax abatement and for the city to provide the parking in a public garage. Meanwhile, the mall developers, who have sapped the vitality of downtown by building shopping centers all around the suburban perimeter, have turned to center city as the last frontier. Their proposal would mean a big jump in sales-tax revenue, but is likely to put many small downtown retailers out of business. A downtown mall will also depend on the city assembling the land, and providing property tax abatement plus publicly financed parking.

More downtown housing would help keep the smaller retailers going, but the downtown housing market is usually limited to young professionals just starting out and a few older people who are tired of caring for a big suburban house and want the convenience of urban living. To compete with suburban alternatives at the low end of the market, developers of new housing want a big land subsidy. Remodeling old downtown loft buildings into apartments used to be supported by federal tax credits. Today developers are saying they would like some tax support from the city.

The city already has a small downtown shopping center, the festival market place on the waterfront. It has not been doing as well as expected, despite a virtual gift of land from the redevelopment authority and favorable mortgage financing through the now defunct federal Urban Development Action Grant program. The owners suggest that the city add an aquarium to attract more people to the waterfront, replicating the combination that has done so well in Baltimore. The aquarium has the enthusiastic support of a blue-ribbon citizens committee, and their consultant has a plan for the largest and most impressive aquarium between Baltimore and Monterey. During the summer months tourists are expected to wander off the interstate at the downtown exit and visit the aquarium in huge numbers, generating more sales taxes and more room tax at a slow time of year for the hotel business. However, under the most favorable attendance projections, the income from admissions will just cover operating expenses. The capital costs will have to be financed some other way.

The baseball team has been getting offers from other cities; the downtown stadium is aging badly and does not have enough of the sky-boxes that are so important to revenue projections these days. The club wants a new ballpark and expects to keep the sky-box revenues for itself.

The highest property values downtown belong to corporate office towers and the headquarters buildings of the local banks and utilities. The president of the city's largest bank was for years the chairman of the downtown business group, and the bank's strong support for downtown was taken for granted. The bank has now been bought by an interstate consortium. The city has been told it is a candidate location for a consolidated operations center, but the bank wants the best deal possible and is talking to several other mayors.

The city obviously can't give everyone everything. Tax abatement is particularly dangerous, as too much, for too long, undermines the whole purpose of encouraging growth in the first place. Other government incentives also have problems. The parking authority has been modestly profitable up to now, but new tax laws have made it more difficult for the authority to put together its own low-cost financing. Increasingly, parking must compete with other city projects like schools and firehouses for an allocation in the capital budget. Capital spending must stay under the city's debt limit, which is, of course, based on the property assessment

Cities got into the business of downtown management gradually, as competition with the suburbs and other metropolitan areas intensified. At first, downtown's problem seemed to be a lack of available land, and cities acquired properties deemed to be blighted, assembled them into development parcels, and often wrote-down the land price using money from the federal government under Title I of the Housing Act of 1949. Some of these urban renewal districts have become successful downtown extensions: Gateway Center in Pittsburgh, Embarcadero Center in San Francisco, Constitution Plaza in Hartford, the Charles Center in Baltimore. The prevailing architectural ideology of the time saw these publicly assembled sites as an opportunity to design a totally new urban environment. With hindsight, even the best of these districts seems too removed from the rest of the city, too many old buildings were torn down, and each new structure was designed separately, and not coordinated with its neighbors. Completion of some urban renewal programs took so long that the whole downtown suffered from having so much empty land. Overenthusiastic land-clearance policies have left holes in some cities that are still unfilled.

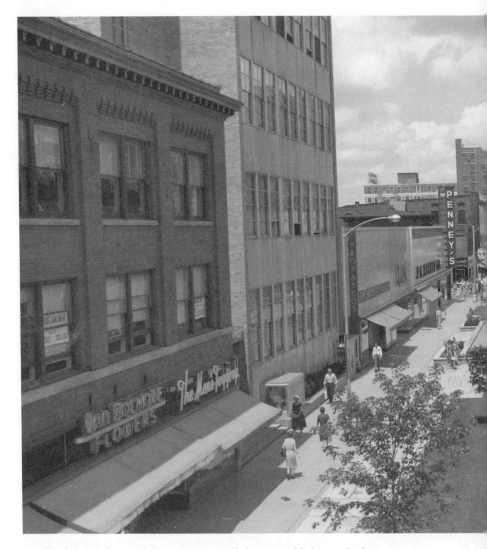

75. *The Burdick Street Mall in downtown Kalamazoo, Michigan, built in accordance with Victor Gruen's 1980 Plan, completed in 1958. At the time,*

More downtown demolition created the highway corridors connecting the old city center to the new interstate system. These connections maintained downtown's role as a regional center, but destroyed so many buildings that they broke up whole districts and gutted neighborhoods. Highway routes were often used to demolish areas the city leadership considered detrimental to economic growth and to separate downtown from places where low-income people lived.

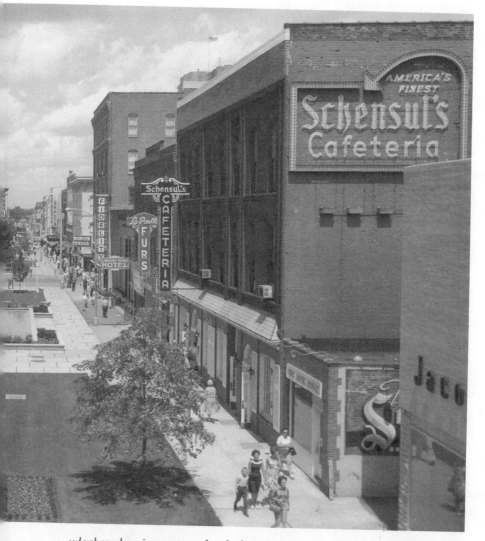

suburban shopping centers often had outdoor malls, so the amenity offered downtown was comparable.

The next phase of downtown renewal was directed not just at providing development sites but toward remaking the city center to compete more effectively with the suburbs. The Burdick Street Mall in Kalamazoo, Michigan, designed by Victor Gruen in 1958, was the first downtown pedestrian mall in the U.S. [75]. Gruen was the architect of several early shopping centers that helped define this new building type. At the time many shopping centers, including Gruen's Northland Center in Detroit, had outdoor malls, so the

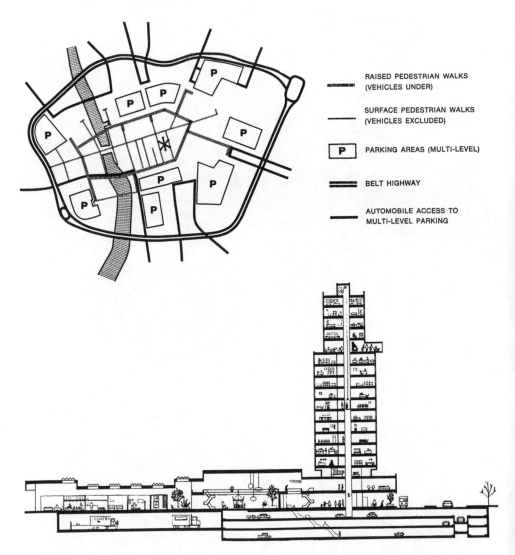

RAISED PEDESTRIAN WALKS
(VEHICLES UNDER)

SURFACE PEDESTRIAN WALKS
(VEHICLES EXCLUDED)

P   PARKING AREAS (MULTI-LEVEL)

BELT HIGHWAY

AUTOMOBILE ACCESS TO
MULTI-LEVEL PARKING

76, 77. *The star marks the location of Midtown Plaza in Rochester, New York. Designed in 1957 according to another plan by Victor Gruen, it was a downtown mixed-use center as shown in the section at right. The relation of the highways to the center is similar to Gruen's 1956 Fort Worth Plan and reflected the then current theory that downtown should be a pedestrian zone, with garages intercepting drivers as they came off the highway.*

Burdick Street design seemed a plausible attempt to duplicate the amenities of the suburbs. Many other communities tried the same tactic. Unfortunately, closing the shopping street to traffic tended to isolate the merchants, and as weather-protected enclosed malls became the suburban norm, the landscaped shopping street was not much of a counterattraction—particularly if there were neither easy access nor enough parking. Many communities, embarrassingly, decided to take the downtown malls back out again, but the failed experiment and two periods of disruptive construction usually meant that there was little retailing left. The pedestrian street has been much more successful in Europe, partly because of the continued preeminence of the European central city, and partly because of strong public transportation systems that continue to bring people into the central district.

Midtown Plaza in Rochester, New York, which opened in 1962, helped define the concept of a downtown enclosed shopping mall. Another Victor Gruen design [76, 77], the new buildings were worked ingeniously into the existing downtown structure, enlarging two existing department stores, providing underground parking and service, and adding two levels of shops plus a combined office building and hotel. Midtown Plaza was small enough so that it did not encompass the whole shopping district; which made it easier to assimilate when it was built, but less effective in preserving Rochester's retail center later on.

Nicollet Mall in Minneapolis, completed in 1967, combined with the Minneapolis skyway system of weather-protected bridges, marked the next stage in the evolution of downtown retailing. The mall has wide sidewalks, but also traffic lanes open to buses, so that the street continues to deliver customers to the front door of the shops. The atrium of the IDS Center, completed in 1973, is a large and attractive indoor space. It is right off the Nicollet Mall, and is also the place where main links of the skyway system intersect, including a bridge into Dayton's, the leading downtown department store. The IDS atrium became the equivalent of an enclosed mall in a shopping center. The skyway system ultimately grew to link 105 buildings and garages on 44 blocks and proved more attractive than the open-air landscaping of the Nicollet Mall, establishing the second floor as the preferred level. Almost all the downtown retail space can now be reached via the skyway system, including several more multilevel mall spaces, notably Gavidae Common and Gavidae Promenade, which have added a group of expensive specialty shops to the downtown retail mix. The Minneapolis transition from street-level access to weather-protected shopping linked at the second floor was carefully managed within the context of a downtown plan that kept stores concentrated in a central area surrounded by a ring of office buildings. Converting downtown from traditional store-front retail to an internal mall inevitably puts some stores out of business and drains life from the streets. The problem for the city is to keep the total amount of retailing as strong as possible, and to try to position the malls so that they will reinforce street-front locations for the kinds of shops that can't afford to be in a mall, or that don't belong there.

The Charles Center in Baltimore is a group of conventional downtown office buildings and hotels, plus a theater and two apartment houses. It was followed by the far more comprehensive Inner Harbor renewal. Demolition for the adjacent Inner Harbor district took out old industrial buildings and piers along the waterfront, as well as a notorious block of bars and X-rated entertainment. What was once a colorful but dark and dangerous low-life district became a sunlit waterfront esplanade, as wholesome as any suburban park. The new waterfront district provided sites for more office buildings and another hotel, but also included the National Aquarium, the Harborplace festival market, and the tall ship U.S.S. *Constellation*. The Inner Harbor project turned Baltimore into a tourist destination and created a thriving downtown district.

However, when it became evident that the shopping along the Inner Harbor had helped finish off the traditional downtown retail locations at Howard and Lexington streets, and undermined the specialty shops leading uptown along Charles Street, the city of Baltimore began to manage the whole downtown comprehensively, rather than assuming it was an essentially successful area that only needed to be shored up in a few selected places.

A similar progression was followed in other cities: government intervention to put together land deals supporting traditional downtown activities; brutal reconstruction to permit highway access;

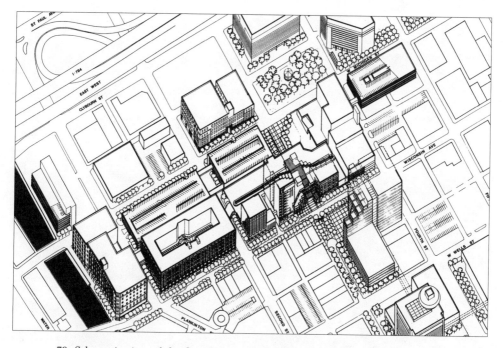

78. Schematic view of the Grand Avenue shopping complex in Milwaukee by the ELS Design Group. A shopping concourse connected existing department stores through an old arcade building. Note, however, how close this successful project is to the entrances and exits of a major highway.

more demolition to remove blight and transform outmoded industrial and warehouse districts into places that would help downtown stay competitive; followed finally by an understanding that downtown needed to be redesigned and managed as a single entity.

The Gallery in Philadelphia is a shopping precinct skillfully inserted into the existing city, with the main shopping concourse one level below grade so that it could make connections under city streets between an existing department store, Strawbridge and Clothier, and a new building for Gimbel's (now a J. C. Penney) several blocks away. While the Gallery with its concentration of stores and associated parking helped keep downtown Philadelphia a retail destination, it still moved much of the activity off Market Street into the internal concourse system.

A similar change in the downtown retail structure was created in Milwaukee at the Grand Avenue project, completed in 1983 [78].

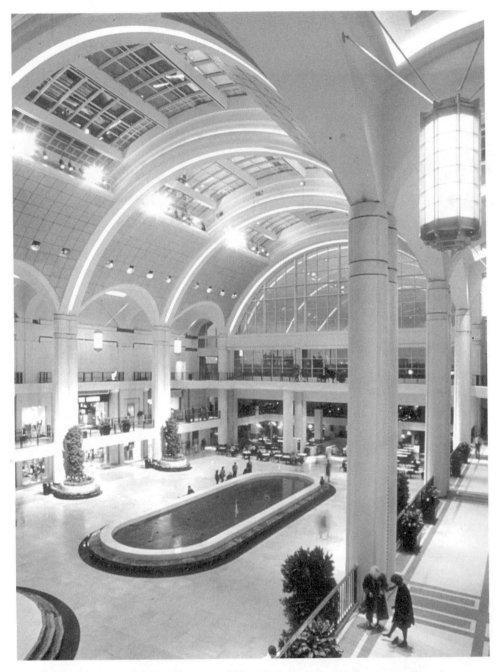

79. *The interior of the Steam Concourse at Tower City in Cleveland, now part of a shopping center designed by RTKL within a landmark railway terminal adjacent to an existing department store. This development has a central location downtown but is also close to exits from the expressway.*

The Plankington Arcade building was remodeled and made part of a concourse system linking two existing downtown department stores. The Grand Avenue was big enough, and close enough to expressway access, to become the dominant mall in the Milwaukee region.

In Cleveland, 350,000 square feet of retailing has been ingeniously inserted next to an existing department store at Tower City [79], an old railway station, office building, retail and hotel complex, which was one of the earliest downtown mixed-use centers, completed in 1929. Although the main retail circulation system is inside, Tower City continues to connect Cleveland's rapid-transit system with Public Square, and care has been taken to maintain strong connections with the downtown street system and a nearby highway interchange.

The Tabor Center in downtown Denver is an interior shopping mall that also keeps in touch with the street environment. A glass-enclosed gallery space is built parallel to Sixteenth Street, Denver's main shopping street. While people move from shop to shop along this internal concourse, they are always in sight of the street, and people walking along the sidewalk can see into the mall.

In good climates, outdoor shopping, particularly for specialty retail, is becoming popular again as people become bored with malls. San Diego's Horton Plaza is a multistory shopping precinct that is actually outdoors, although clearly separated from the downtown street system. John Jerde's design mixes the organization of a conventional shopping mall with the atmosphere of festival market places, which usually have at least some outdoor circulation, following the lead of Ghirardelli Square and the Cannery in San Francisco, or Quincy Market in Boston.

The proposed Bay City Plaza in St. Petersburg, Florida, would integrate new retail into the downtown street system and avoid enclosing all the stores in an interior shopping concourse. Parking decks above department stores would bring shoppers close to their destination; circulation from store to store could take place both on second-level bridges and along sidewalks lined with active street frontages [80, 81, 82].

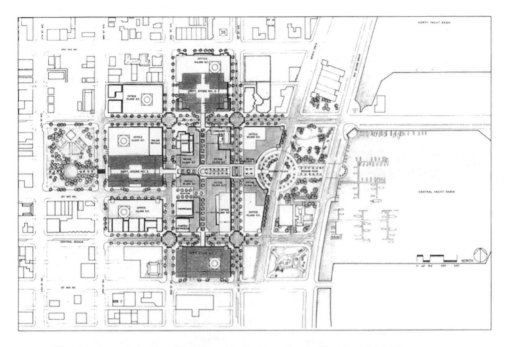

80. The plan of the Bay City Plaza in St. Petersburg, Florida, which, if completed, would introduce new retail into downtown streets without enclosing all the stores in an interior shopping concourse. Parking decks above department stores and offices permit active street frontages; second-level bridges make other necessary pedestrian connections.

Most downtowns also have a gaslight district of restaurants, entertainment, and highly discretionary shopping. The Vieux Carré in New Orleans is a genuine historic district that functions as a regional, and even national, destination for jazz and good food in a setting of architectural interest. In many other cities the comparable area is more artificial, created from old warehouse and industrial buildings whose attraction is their cheap space as much as their architectural character. Shockoe Slip in Richmond, the Flats in Cleveland, Pioneer Square in Seattle, and Larimer Square in Denver are representative examples and have comparable histories. A few preservationists and entrepreneurs saw the possibilities, and their investment was later backed up by city policies. It is one of the most heartening signs for the continued survival of older urban centers that people will drive downtown after work, or be attracted to a convention, because these districts are more interesting and more fun than looking for food and entertainment along the highway near the mall.

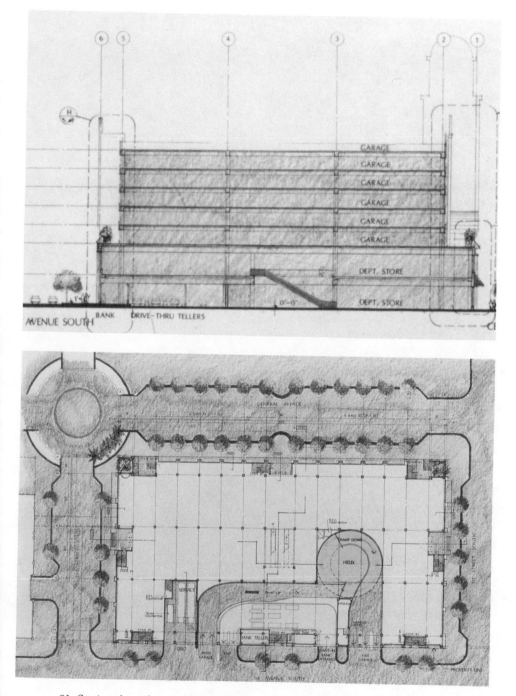

81. *Section through one of the department stores shows parking above.*

82. *Plan shows parking ramp in relation to the ground floor of the department store.*

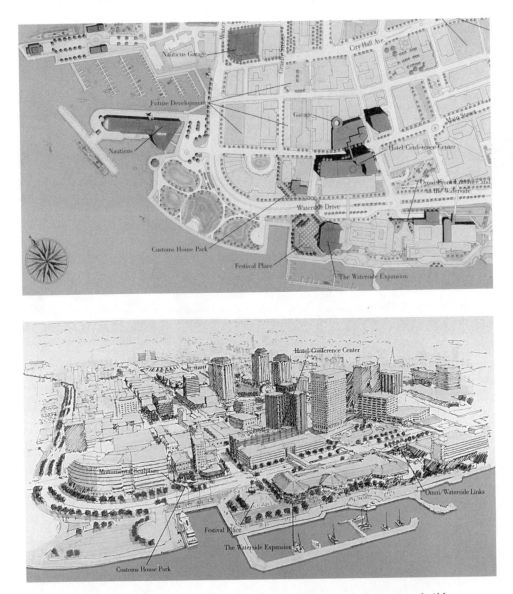

*83, 84, 85. Norfolk, Virginia, has pursued an entrepreneurial strategy to rebuild
the downtown waterfront so that it can attract convention visitors and tourists.
Redevelopment has created a festival marketplace, two convention hotels and a
convention center, a nautical museum, and the Freemason Harbor residential
neighborhood. 1980 plan by Wallace Roberts and Todd; 1990 plan by Philip
Hammer, UDA Architects, Jonathan Barnett.*

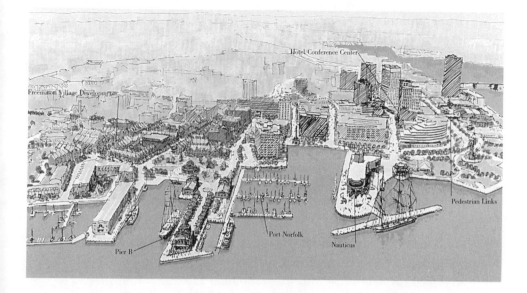

Downtown malls, festival markets, and gaslight districts have all required extensive government intervention to put the land together and help with the financing and parking. Intervention to support downtown retailing leads logically to public support for other attractions that will increase the number of visitors: a convention center; an aquarium or other downtown museum; a downtown performing arts center; a downtown stadium plus a civic arena for basketball, hockey, and concerts—even riverboat gambling—all intended to draw more visitors and suburbanites, especially on evenings and weekends. The Baltimore Aquarium and the new Camden Yards Stadium for the Baltimore Orioles are two influential examples. Amazingly decorated old vaudeville theaters, often shuttered for years, have been restored as new homes for symphonies, ballet, opera, and legitimate theater, like Heinz Hall and the Benedum Center in Pittsburgh or Playhouse Square in Cleveland. Alternatively, cities have built new performing arts centers in or near downtown, like the new hall for the San Francisco Symphony.

Norfolk, Virginia, is an example of a community that has almost completely remade its downtown in order to remain a regional center. It built one of the first civic arenas and supports an art museum, a nautical museum, a concert hall, an opera, and a repertory theater. It has rebuilt its waterfront to attract convention visitors and tourists, creating a festival marketplace, two convention hotels and a convention center, a nautical museum, and a new downtown baseball stadium. The city has also extended and improved a downtown residential neighborhood [83, 84, 85].

Almost every city has sought to strengthen historic downtown residential districts and add other, new neighborhoods in order to provide a 24-hour base for downtown retail and restaurants, keep downtown streets peopled after business hours to provide a sense of safety, and make downtown office space more attractive for business.

The Society Hill neighborhood in downtown Philadelphia was redeveloped at the same time that urban renewal efforts in other cities produced clusters of downtown residential towers. Authorities in Philadelphia proceeded far more selectively, ensuring the preservation and restoration of many of the old, if modest, houses in the area. Much of the new residential building took the form of low-scale, in-fill buildings, and the three new apartment towers were sited to be an architectural accent, rather than a random disruption. As a result, Society Hill has the atmosphere of traditional downtown neighborhoods, like Beacon Hill and the Back Bay in Boston, that did not require extensive urban renewal.

The Ghent Square neighborhood in Norfolk [86] is another area close to a downtown that was redeveloped as a traditional residential neighborhood, and not as a new world of towers and plazas. Old buildings were restored, and reinforced by small in-fill buildings. The cleared land was planned around a new square, with limits on the height of new buildings so that a traditional scale was maintained.

Such new neighborhoods are naturally far more expensive to live in than the rundown buildings they replace. At neither Society Hill nor Ghent did the old residents have much of an opportunity to return. The reinforcement that an in-town middle- to upper-income neighborhood gives to the stability of the downtown is the justification for using public funds to effect such a social change.

Quality Hill in downtown Kansas City [87], an area so run-down and

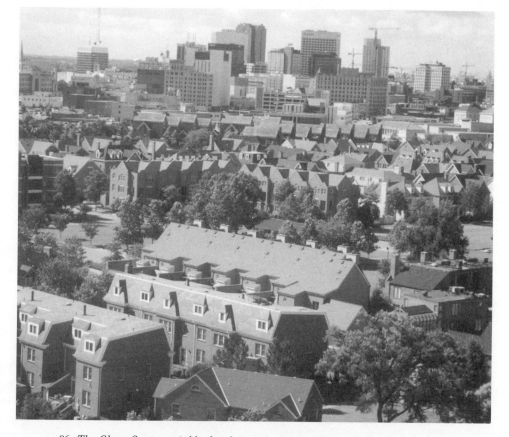

86. *The Ghent Square neighborhood near downtown Norfolk supports downtown redevelopment by providing middle- and upper-income housing in what was once a deteriorating low-income area. It has taken the Norfolk Housing and Redevelopment Authority a generation of continuous effort to develop the original plan by Harry Weese & Associates.*

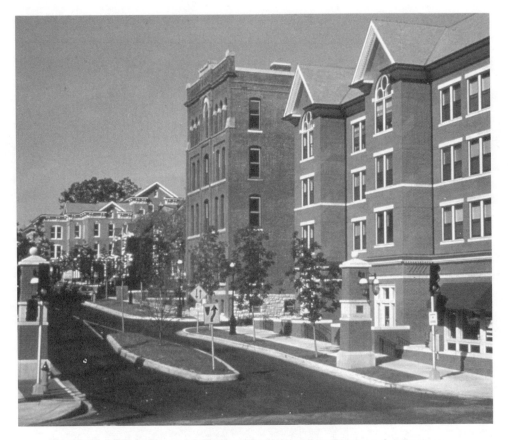

*87. Quality Hill in downtown Kansas City also supports downtown by creating a
moderate- and middle-income neighborhood. Financing required revenue bonds,
an Urban Development Action Grant, funds from the City, and special community
loan funds, in addition to the 27 percent of the cost invested by limited partners.*

deserted that it required little relocation of existing residents, is a recent example of a new downtown residential neighborhood created on something like the Society Hill pattern.

Other close-in residential neighborhoods that were once mansion districts for the rich have benefited from new investment as they have become a preferred location for small professional offices, elegant small apartments, and, sometimes, for houses of wealthy people. Calling this phenomenon gentrification is a wry acknowledgment that it is not an unmixed blessing: the city's tax base and downtown are strengthened, but low-income people who were tenants in the buildings before renovation are usually displaced to other locations.

As cities assumed more and more responsibility for downtown they began to see the need to spend money on civic design and urban beautification. In order to compete effectively against attractive suburbs, cities have been forced to create new parks, improve street furniture, landscape streets, and manage the appearance of new buildings through zoning controls and design review.

Sometimes redesigning the city center has required major investment as well as coordinated design and management policies. Portland, Oregon, was the first major city to remove an expressway that had been constructed to improve access to the city center. The highway that cut downtown off from the Willamette River was demolished in the early 1970s and replaced with a park. San Franciscans had succeeded in stopping the extension of the Embarcadero Freeway around the downtown waterfront, and now the stub of the expressway has been removed [88, 89, 90], permitting a newly landscaped boulevard and much better connections between the city and the waterfront. In Boston, the Fitzgerald Expressway, which sliced the North End and the waterfront away from the business center, is to be replaced by an underground highway that is part of a series of road, bridge, and tunnel improvements expected to cost $7.2 billion. Devoting expenditure at this level to improvements whose justification is as much visual as functional is a remarkable transformation of the way engineering is done in cities [91]. The potential value of the park and building sites to be created by putting the highway underground in downtown Boston can be

88, 89. *The removal of the Embarcadero Freeway in San Francisco reverses a controversial decision to put traffic movement ahead of city design and permits the creation of a new setting by the ROMA Design Group for the landmark Ferry Building.*

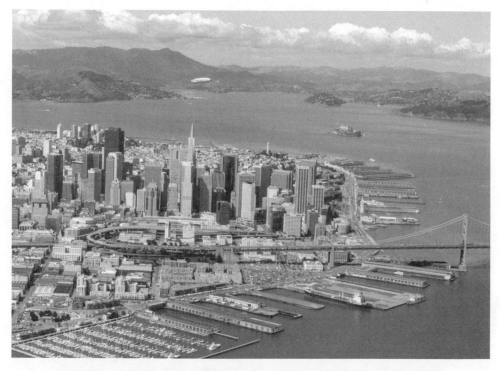

90. Aerial view of downtown San Francisco after the Embarcadero Freeway was removed shows the new development being created along the waterfront south of Market Street.

estimated by looking at the benefits the riverfront park system has created in downtown San Antonio [92–95].

The 1980s saw a major office-building boom in city centers as financial service companies grew and added new clerical workers. A few cities, like San Francisco, sought to moderate the growth of the downtown skyline, but most cities welcomed it. Because downtown property ownership is often fragmented, putting parcels together through urban renewal can still promote development that would have not taken place otherwise. Land subsidy is not necessarily needed; it is the creation of the parcel that makes the difference. Cities continue to use tax abatement, low-interest loans, publicly financed parking garages, and tax-increment financing of public amenities to spur private investment in city centers. As the battle for survival intensifies, more and more development incentives come into play. Even cities like New York and Chicago that have

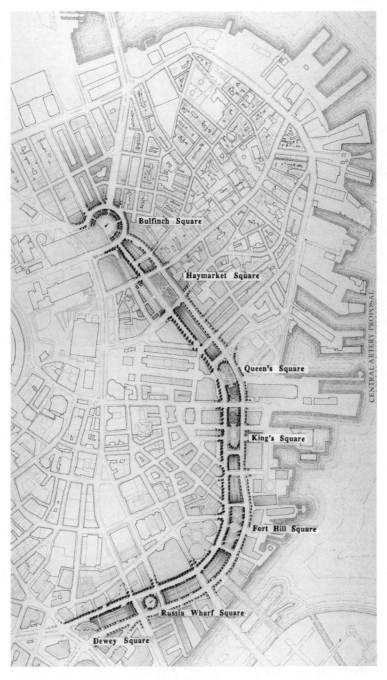

91. *The replacement of Boston's elevated Central Artery with an underground highway creates the opportunity for a sequence of parks and development sites that will knit the fabric of downtown Boston back together. Plan by Chan, Krieger, Levi Architects, for the Boston Redevelopment Authority.*

seldom used incentives in their central business districts are beginning to find them necessary.

Downtown improvement districts are both a heartening sign that some business interests remain committed to the center city, and a warning signal that cities are no longer fulfilling their primary responsibilities. Essentially, an improvement district is an additional taxing jurisdiction, within which property owners agree to contribute to a special fund that is used to maintain extra security and other services like street-cleaning. Improvement districts began as a means of maintaining special lighting and landscaping on downtown shopping streets. Today, however, in midtown Manhattan there is a mosaic of business improvement districts that do such things as help take care of homeless people, maintain a park, and provide squads of extra sanitation workers, as well as financing special street-lighting, newsstands, trees, and other amenities.

Improvement districts are created by New York City, under enabling legislation from the state, with the consent of a major percentage of the property owners in the designated area. The property owners are saying, in effect, that they are sick of subsidizing the rest of the city and not getting much back. They are willing to pay a little more, but want all of it used for the district's benefit. The district is thus an implicit brake on the ability of the city to raise the general tax rate. Tax increment financing districts, used in many cities to finance improvements for specific areas, have a similar effect.

Despite overall growth in the U.S. economy, downtown management is becoming an increasingly sophisticated zero-sum game. When Minneapolis built a new downtown baseball stadium for the Twins, the suburb of Bloomington retaliated by redeveloping the site of the former baseball stadium as the 4-million-square-foot Mall of America. The Minneapolis metropolitan area is one of the few places in the United States to have genuine regional revenue sharing. But even in this enlightened environment, Bloomington used close to a quarter of a billion dollars in public money to improve roadways and utilities and build 13,000 garage parking spaces for a shopping center certain to undermine the retail districts of Minneapolis, St. Paul, and other surrounding municipalities.

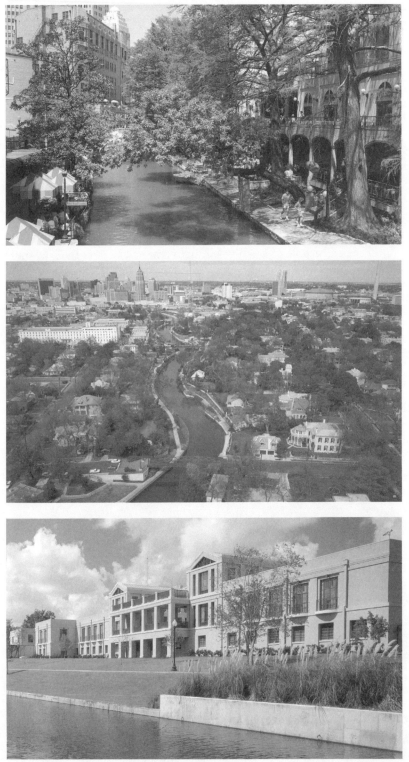

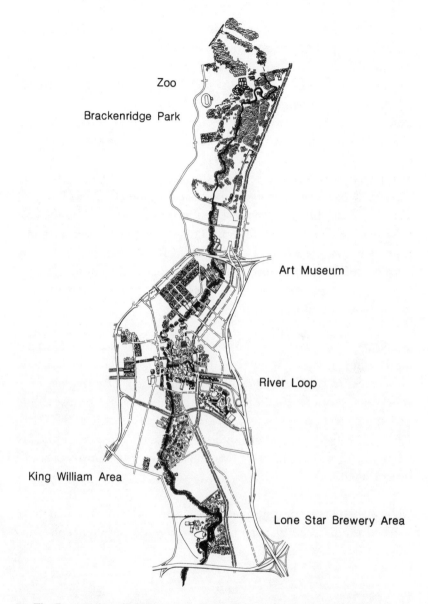

Zoo

Brackenridge Park

Art Museum

River Loop

King William Area

Lone Star Brewery Area

92. *The Riverwalk in San Antonio began downtown as a WPA project in the 1930s.*

93. *It has since been greatly extended, providing a landscaped setting for old neighborhoods and new buildings.*

94. *The headquarters of the HEB Grocery Company, designed by Hartman-Cox Architects, includes renovations and additions to an old armory complex and fronts on the Riverwalk south of downtown.*

95. *Skidmore Owings and Merrill's plan uses the Riverwalk as a catalyst for new development (above).*

Imagine again that you are a mayor, and you are now informed that many property assessments downtown will have to be reduced again because of vacant office space and slowing retail business. The vacancy rate for office space is going down, but downtown tenants are not hiring the way they did in the 1980s and have become more astute about using less space to house more workers through such techniques as high-density filing, and shared office space ("hotelling") for employees who are only in the office some of the time. There is thus not much demand for new office towers that would expand the tax base. The downtown improvement districts have put a cap on your ability to raise the real estate tax rate, while the cost of providing city services continues to go up. Raising tax rates in a time of falling commercial assessments also shifts more of the tax burden to residential property, including single-family houses whose owners can be expected to vote against the politician who is raising their tax burden.

While recent management improvements have made city agencies more efficient and productive, the unions and the entrenched bureaucracies continue to resist attempts to use city money more effectively. An attempt to let private companies bid on providing garbage collection and street repair is tied up in litigation. There seems to be little the mayor can do but cut back on services and lay off city staff, despite the risk that more people and businesses will leave the city.

Older urban areas, despite their many accomplishments, may have reached the limit of their ability to survive through entrepreneurship.

7

Bypassed Areas:
The New Urban Frontier

While downtowns have been growing, the rest of the city has been shrinking. Old-style multistory factory buildings have been abandoned, piers along harbors and riverfronts are no longer used, and many railway yards are empty.

A few cities like New York and Los Angeles are gateways for immigration; as people leave, they are replaced by new arrivals. Many other U.S. cities have seen big drops in population, resulting in large areas of vacant land and deserted, burned-out buildings. Some cities have grown substantially, but most of the growth has taken place in new areas added to the city limits by annexation or consolidation with surrounding counties. While Houston grew by 174 percent between 1950 and 1990, it has older, inner-city areas as rundown and deserted as neighborhoods in Detroit. Detroit officials have been talking seriously about decanting people from sparsely populated neighborhoods into more settled areas and turning off municipal services in whole sections of the city.

Deserted buildings and neighborhoods are evidence of tragic loss, but they also represent opportunities. Their location and services could be valuable assets, because land that has a current real estate value of almost nothing is equipped with water, sewer, gas, and electricity services that would cost a lot of money to duplicate in a greenfield location on the urban fringe.

In 1976, the architect Robert Stern prepared a project for the Venice Biennale entitled Subway Suburb [96]. It showed the redevelopment of several large vacant blocks in New York City's borough of the Bronx with a mix of garden apartments around courtyards, two-family houses, and small, affordable single-family houses. While the houses all have garages, the drawing shows that it is only a short walk to a transit station on a line leading to the

Manhattan skyline in the background. The intent of these drawings was polemical. No one at the time was proposing this kind of comprehensive renewal, much less for middle-income families, although there were actual development sites available in the Bronx at this scale. Today, ad hoc in-fill and rehab efforts have removed the possibility of inventing whole new neighborhoods in the Bronx, but there are many other cities where a development like this would be possible.

The politics of such a change are admittedly tricky. People who still live in bypassed inner-city neighborhoods are well aware of the area's real estate potential and are on guard against being shunted aside to make room for suburbanites.

So far, the closest approach to Stern's Subway Suburb has been achieved at places like Ghent, near downtown Norfolk, Virginia, and Quality Hill in downtown Kansas City, described in chapter 6. These relatively upscale neighborhoods were created by government actions designed to reinforce the downtown economy. In many cases poor residents of such districts have been moved out to make way for the new development. While a strong public policy argument can be made for anything that strengthens downtown, this type of in-town suburb is not a prototype for all inner city areas.

The redevelopment of large sections of the Hill District in Pittsburgh creates a new suburban environment designed to serve the population of an area that has been a low-income black neighborhood for a long time. It is closer to the model of the Subway Suburb, although it is actually within walking distance of the city center [97, 98].

The current market for a new suburb in derelict parts of an old city is likely to consist of people from nearby areas who have started to make a little money, plus people whose other housing choice is a small house or a mobile-home way out on the urban fringe. To eliminate long hours of commuting every day, they might be willing to consider a house in a close-in neighborhood, but the neighborhood has to be affordable and part of an area large enough, and complete enough, to be clearly distinguishable from deteriorated inner-city districts.

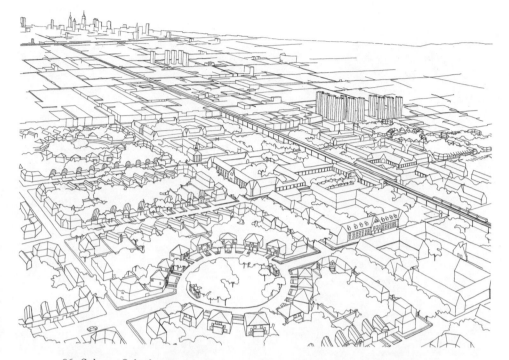

96. *Subway Suburb project by Robert A. M. Stern illustrating the potential of deserted inner-city areas for new suburban-style development.*

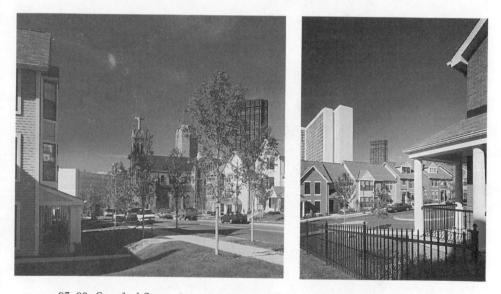

97, 98. *Crawford Square is a new development in Pittsburgh's Hill District, the scene of* Fences *and several other plays by August Wilson. It includes housing priced so that residents of the area can continue to live there. The plan is by UDA Architects.*

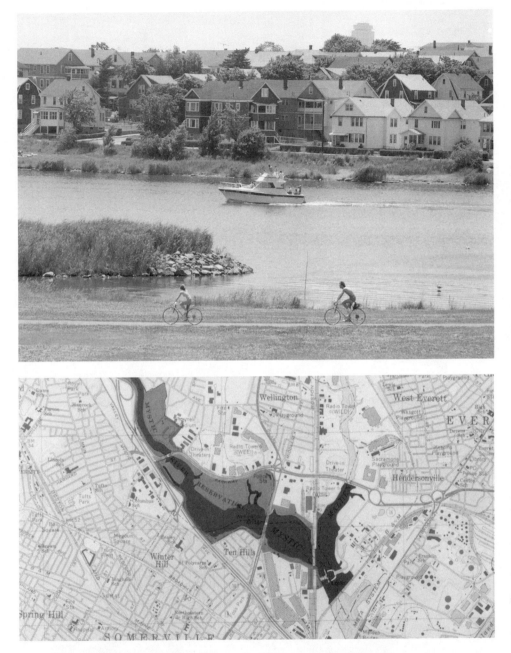

99, 100. *The design by Carol Johnson & Associates for the Mystic River Reservation near Boston creates a riverfront park from contaminated and sterile land, once used for industry and then abandoned. The park is a new setting for existing urban neighborhoods, which suddenly have many of the advantages of suburban communities. (The top of Boston's Prudential tower is just visible in the distance.)*

At a Regional Plan Association conference on the future of the inner city, a real estate developer was asked what the first move should be in making a bypassed urban area an attractive alternative to suburbia. His answer: "Build a golf course." The prescription makes sense, despite its shock value. If old neighborhoods are to be alternatives to suburbia, they need to offer comparable amenities, although a golf course is not the only possibility.

The map in Illustration 100 shows 200 acres along the Mystic River near Boston, typical of riverfront land in older American cities: derelict industrial sites, mostly built on fill dredged out of the river and harbor, sliced by expressways. When Carol Johnson & Associates were retained to turn this area into parkland, much of the soil was toxic to plants. The ground was made into a growing medium by blending layers of clay, silt, sand, and peat, without importing topsoil stripped from other locations. In the first stage, 80 acres were redeveloped at a cost of $5,000,000. The transformation of the riverfront gives houses in an urban Somerville neighborhood a setting comparable to choice locations much farther out in suburbia, as shown in the photograph [99], while the park itself is an amenity rarely found in close-in urban neighborhoods.

Old factory districts represent another large category of bypassed urban land. Success in reusing these sites has depended so far on where they are located. Thousands of acres of old steel mills still languish in the Monongahela Valley southeast of Pittsburgh, while the old Jones and Laughlin mill that is closer to the city center, and right down the hill from Carnegie Mellon and the University of Pittsburgh, is being redeveloped as the Pittsburgh Technology Center.

In New York City's cast-iron district, where conditions were once so bad it was called Hell's Hundred Acres, streets of old loft buildings have been reborn as SoHo, a fashionable art, residential, and commercial quarter. Similar transformations of downtown loft districts have taken place in other cities, with the degree of success depending on demand for the alternate living and work environments possible in a loft. Generally the bigger the city, the greater the demand. Printing House Square in Chicago is the successful renovation of a substantial area, while the warehouse district in

Cleveland, the Garment District in downtown Kansas City, or the Lowertown redevelopment in St. Paul represent significant change, but are still struggling.

There are some older, small cities that had old manufacturing buildings of comparable character and historical interest to the loft districts in big cities. In the 1970s, Lowell, Massachusetts, situated on the Merrimack River northeast of Boston, looked like a community that had no future. The textile businesses that had made it a thriving manufacturing center had moved to the south, or to other countries. Former Massachusetts Senator Paul Tsongas, a native of Lowell who had been a Lowell city councilman, succeeded in persuading the U.S. Congress to pass legislation making parts of old industrial Lowell an urban national park. The National Park Service, somewhat to its surprise, found that Lowell had a good claim to being the place where the industrial revolution started in the United States. Following a plan devised by the urban design firm Lane, Frenchman Associates, buildings were restored and exhibitions prepared, and Lowell became a tourist attraction. The tourists helped create a modest revival of local service businesses like restaurants.

Then there was a dramatic development. The Boston metropolitan area had grown out past Lowell, and An Wang, the founder of the Wang computer company, was looking for sites for his fast-growing company. He settled on Lowell, took over some of the old textile factory buildings, and constructed a new corporate headquarters. Lowell's future seemed assured. Recently, in another dramatic turn of events, Wang computer products have fallen on bad times, and the future of Wang is in doubt.

In the meantime, the principle of using industrial history to underpin the economy of small, older cities was being applied in other places. The state of Massachusetts started a program of state historic parks in six old manufacturing cities, including Lawrence, another old mill town near Lowell, and New Bedford, a small seaport on Buzzards Bay, west of Cape Cod. Heritage parks are also being planned for old industrial and mining areas in central Pennsylvania [101, 102].

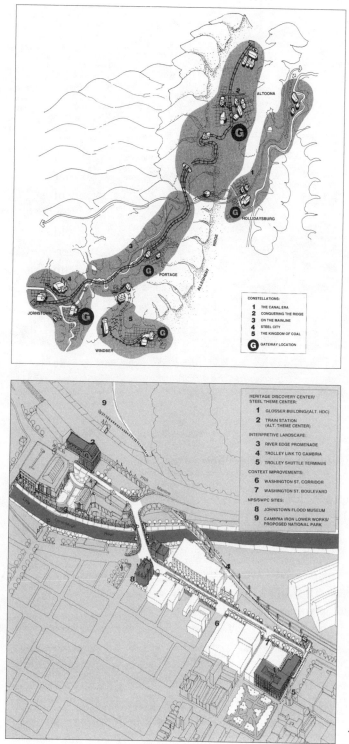

101. *A plan by Lane, Frenchman Associates for creating tourist attractions from disused industrial sites in central Pennsylvania.*

102. *Detail of Area G in the previous illustration. The heritage park concept was first used successfully in the National Park at Lowell, Massachusetts, where Lane, Frenchman were the master planners for the National Park Service.*

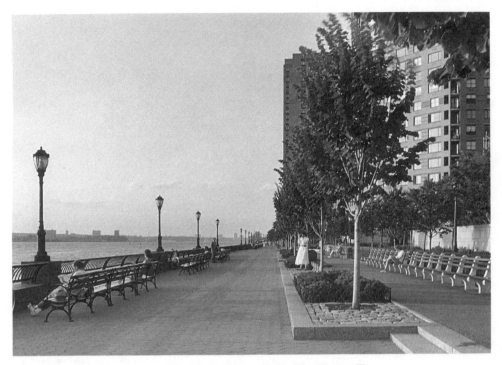

103. *The esplanade at Battery Park City in Lower Manhattan. The master planners, Cooper, Eckstut, sought to replicate the atmosphere of older Manhattan neighborhoods. The landscape architects were Hanna, Olin.*

Paterson, New Jersey, is another early industrial city that has used its history and inventory of old buildings as the basis for a renewal strategy, so far with only limited success compared to Waterbury, Connecticut, strategically located on the fashionable side of both New York and Hartford, which has found a strong market for old manufacturing structures as corporate office buildings.

There are plenty of old loft and factory buildings no longer in demand for large-scale modern manufacturing and located in areas where they are not readily converted to other uses by the current real estate market. One possible use for these buildings is as incubators for new manufacturing businesses. Cheap space is one incentive, but what is also needed is a management support system to help new business get started. Building or renovating structures to support new industries in cities is a well-established policy in France and, to a lesser degree, in England, but is still a new idea in the United States. One U.S. example is the manufacturing center in

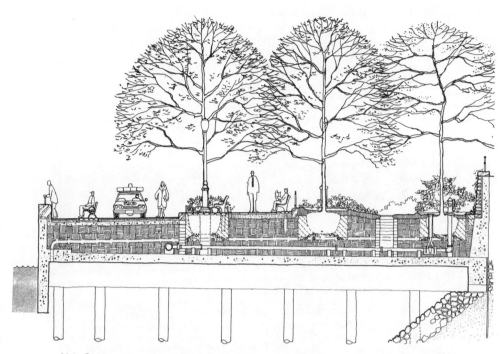

104. Cross-section of the Battery Park City esplanade.

Charleston, South Carolina, organized by the Control Data corporation; another is the Technology Center in New Haven, developed within buildings left behind by the Olin Corporation. A policy of developing business incubators in older urban districts relates well to the concept of urban enterprise or empowerment zones, where businesses can be given tax abatements and relief from certain regulations.

Another possible use for old industrial buildings is housing. Housing reformers have usually ignored the potential of these structures because they are large and thus hard to manage, and they do not meet modern code requirements for residences. City governments are also reluctant to change zoning designations and admit that industrial jobs are gone forever. However, as upper-middle-class people are willing to live in downtown lofts, the reuse of old factories for housing is worth a second look. The existence of a sound structural envelope may help make such housing affordable. One possibility is self-help housing, in which the loft is purchased with rough plumbing and electrical systems in place, and the tenants do the rest. This is how many artists and young professional people have renovated lofts in cities. Another possibility is to remodel factories or warehouses as congregate housing for the elderly, or for any other group-living option that requires a built-in management structure in any case, and thus can deal with large, complicated buildings.

Many piers and waterfront railway marshaling yards are no longer needed for industry, and the land is often derelict and polluted. American cities have been cut off from their waterfronts by freight and industrial uses; redevelopment provides an opportunity to give buildings the advantage of waterfront views and access, and bring the public back to the water's edge.

The future of these waterfront industrial areas has depended so far on the real estate market in nearby areas. The West Side piers adjacent to the skyscrapers of lower Manhattan have become Battery Park City, two residential neighborhoods bordering on an office and shopping center. The idea was first proposed in the Lower Manhattan Plan of 1965, prepared by Conklin and Rossant in association with Wallace, McHarg, Roberts & Todd. The plan that was actually followed, after a number of false starts, was prepared by Cooper, Eckstut in 1979 [103, 104]. The development will probably be complete early in the next century.

Battery Park City's urban design strategy, creating new residential neighborhoods according to traditional patterns, has been a model for other recent large-scale reclamation projects in cities, whether piers or railway yards. Instead of treating the whole site as an area free of streets, as at the Prudential Center in Boston, built over a railway yard in the early 1960s, the site is divided into blocks that extend the surrounding street network. Parks and vistas are integrated into the street system to provide a variety of experiences. The waterfront is not treated as the private preserve of individual buildings but separated from development by a boulevard, which gives access to a waterfront park or esplanade.

The Mission Bay redevelopment in San Francisco [105, 106], the

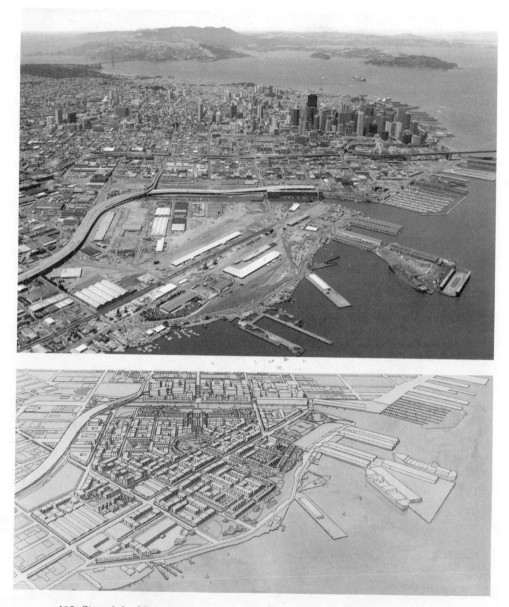

105. Site of the Mission Bay development in San Francisco, with the downtown skyline in the background.

106. The plan for Mission Bay by Skidmore Owings & Merrill, the latest in a series of plans by several different consultants, reflects recent thinking that such bypassed areas should become new residential neighborhoods, not self-contained "new towns, in-town." Note the removal of the elevated roadway, which permits better integration with the downtown street system.

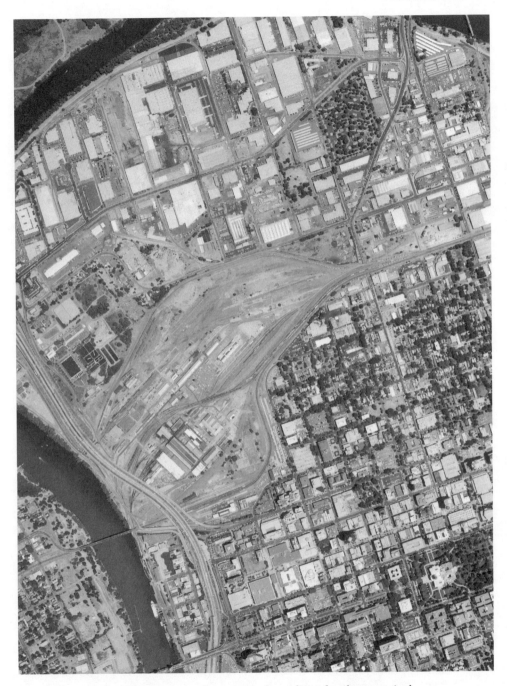

107. *Aerial view of downtown Sacramento shows disused railway repair shops and marshaling yards. The state capitol is in the lower right-hand corner of the photograph.*

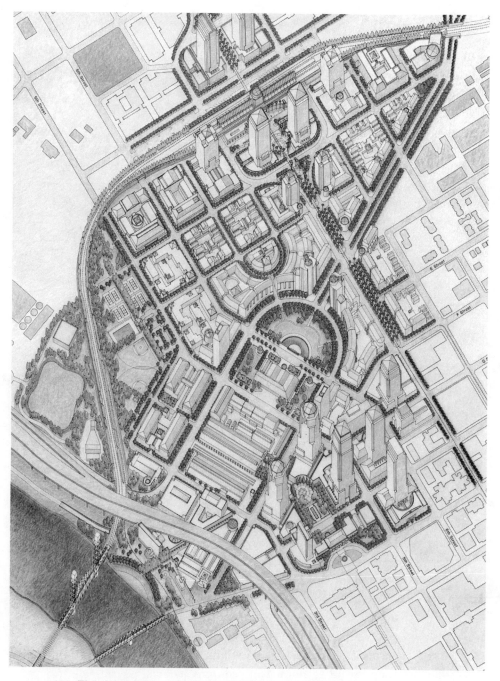

108. *The plan for the yards, by the ROMA Design Group, creates a new downtown residential district and two clusters of office buildings, with commercial uses in the old repair shops, which are to be preserved as significant historical buildings.*

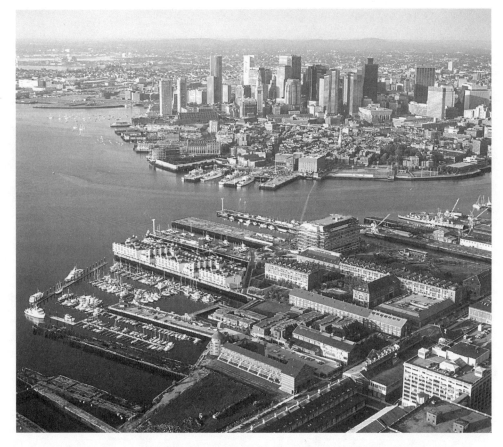

109. Aerial view of the Charlestown Navy Yard, in Boston Harbor, converted over a 20-year period to a mix of office, research, and residential uses.

redevelopment of the Union Pacific yards in Sacramento [107, 108], and the Riverside South redevelopment of the Sixtieth Street railway yards on Manhattan's Upper West Side are all examples of long-term plans for the reclamation of major pieces of urban property as new urban neighborhoods.

Military bases occupy prime locations in many American cities and towns. Eliminating military installations that are becoming redundant is a painful hit to the urban economy as local payrolls disappear and military personnel move away, but many of these bases are tremendous long-term real estate opportunities. The Charlestown Navy Yard in Boston Harbor is a good example; its redevelopment

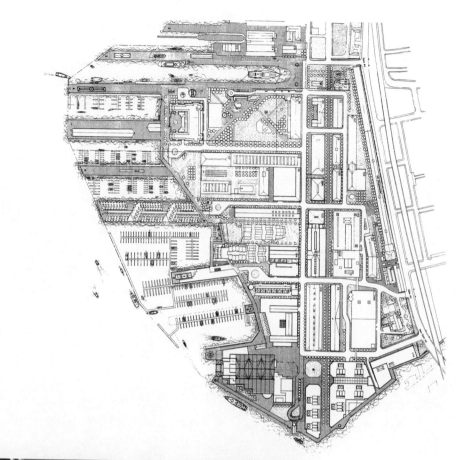

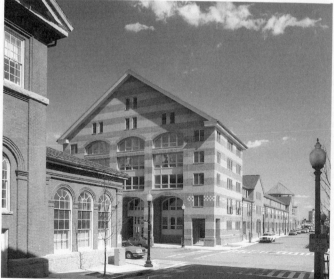

110. *The illustrative site plan shows ultimate build-out of the Navy Yard. Anderson, Notter, Feingold were the master planners for the Boston Redevelopment Authority.*

111. *Moderate-income housing in the Charlestown Navy Yard designed by William Rawn & Associates to relate to the character of historic structures in the Yard.*

was aided by the fact that many of its installations were historic buildings [109, 110, 111].

Vacant residential blocks, empty lofts and factories, unneeded railway yards, and derelict piers exist in almost every older city. Prototypes for the reclamation of these areas now exist, so that many of the technical design problems have been solved. What is missing now are the financial mechanisms to support long-term redevelopment in cities.

Restricting growth at the urban fringe and making improvements in bypassed parts of the older city are interdependent policies. Growth restraints at the fringe make bypassed areas a more significant alternative, but only if a decisive effort makes new investment possible.

8

Restoring Communities

I n many old cities there are large areas where people who have
any choice at all refuse to live. Conditions there are becoming
worse and worse. Housing is deteriorating, jobs within commuting distance are hard to find, the schools are increasingly inef-
fective and dangerous, city services are going downhill, law and
order are breaking down. These areas are both a cause and a consequence of the fragmenting of cities. As new cities grow, these parts
of the old city become even more cut off from the rest of society,
making conditions worse, and causing more strain on the social and
physical fabric of the old city, which sets off another round of
people and businesses leaving for new locations.

The problems of these inner-city areas have continued for generations, despite the efforts of social reformers and government programs; obviously, there are no simple answers. But no lasting solution to the other problems of cities and suburbs is possible unless
this one is solved as well. As long as such conditions persist, the
economic health of the old city will still be in jeopardy and the
ecological damage and gridlock of uncontrolled metropolitan expansion will continue.

Inner-city areas where squalor and crime are concentrated are not
an inevitable consequence of modern urban life. Canada and Australia somehow manage their societies without urban problems at
this scale, as do the Scandinavian countries, the Netherlands, Singa-
pore, and Japan. While experts differ, the most generally accepted
explanation for what is happening to these inner-city districts in the
United States is a breakdown of community—that is, all the problems of housing, jobs, schools, drug-use, health-care, and crime are
interrelated and thus each of them makes the others worse.

In 1965 the administration of President Lyndon Johnson proposed the Model Cities program, in which one neighborhood in each of three representative cities would be the subject of comprehensive programs, funded as required, as a demonstration that such areas could be transformed. People would be empowered to take control of the future of their neighborhood by participating in all planning decisions. There would be programs to remodel existing housing and build new housing units, but there would also be programs to improve schools and provide vocational training for adults, health services targeting the needs of the community, special efforts to improve city services to the area, and so on. In order to get the Model Cities program through the Congress, 3 demonstrations became 66 and then 150; at the same time, the U.S. commitment to the war in Vietnam began to escalate.

The preliminary organizing for Model Cities was done: committees were formed in the communities; public meetings were held; decisions were debated; compromises and plans were hammered out— often after unpleasant conflicts between community activists and government officials used to doing things the old way. In the end, overcommitment in too many cities, and the draining of all available funds into the war in Vietnam, meant that there was nowhere near the amount of money needed to carry out these ambitious programs. Instead of demonstrating what could be done for a community, the program demonstrated how to raise expectations and then demolish them, leaving people feeling angrier and more hopeless than they had been before. Model Cities is remembered as a failure, but no one knows how effective it might have been if fully funded.

Model Cities sought to make amends for earlier high-handed city policies by treating inner city residents as a group with community interests and values. It probably did not give enough emphasis to the stress such communities are under, and thus the difficulty of solving their problems by working solely within their own geographic area. Thirty years later these stresses have grown worse; it is no longer possible to solve the problems of inner city districts without integrating them into a larger community.

As discussed in chapter 4, the nature of community is a subtle issue, but most people are clear what the minimum requirements are to foster a community: affordable housing, public safety, and effective schools. There are, of course, some other basic requirements that are usually taken for granted: utilities and streets, garbage and trash collection, fire protection, mail delivery and other government services. A pleasant environment is also desirable, as are recreation space and suitable locations for community institutions.

For years slum clearance was thought to be the first step in restoring urban areas. Many urban slums were ramshackle collections of wooden structures, often with no indoor plumbing; others were airless tenements built before building codes were enacted. The public housing that replaced the slums was deliberately planned as a temporary holding area for poor people, who were expected to move out as soon as "they got back on their feet." This policy was begun during the Great Depression of the 1930s and may have made sense then; it does not make sense now when public housing is clearly a permanent home for many people.

The breakdown of community, and law and order, is built into the design of many housing projects. Repetitive identical buildings where an apartment location is only recognizable by number, confusing street layouts, public spaces where security is impossible, all these design defects can be corrected; so can the management defect that limited occupancy in these buildings to people with the lowest incomes.

In many cities, 10 percent or more of dwellings are located in public housing, and integrating this housing into a permanent community should be a priority everywhere.

One of the most extensive conversions of a public housing project has been the transformation of the Columbia Point housing in Boston to a mixed income community [112]. The street plan was completely revised to replace dangerously confusing, winding streets with a grid plan and a central community mall [113, 114]. Many of the original housing towers were demolished to make way for town houses and mid-rise buildings. The result is a well-maintained place where a wide variety of people can live, instead of a series of crime-ridden, impersonal warehouses only for low-income tenants.

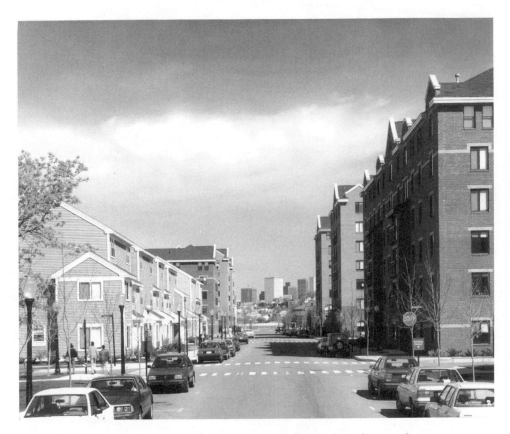

112. *The transformation of Boston's notorious Columbia Point housing from a
badly deteriorated, almost empty series of barrackslike buildings into a
mixed-income community is a prototype for changing housing projects into
neighborhoods. Above, a street scene in the now transformed project.*

At the Lake Parc Place project in Chicago, law and order had
broken down completely and the buildings were controlled by street
gangs. The Chicago Housing Authority vacated and remodeled
Lake Parc, which is now managed by a private real estate company
as a mixed-income community with nearly equal numbers of welfare recipients and working families. Prospective tenants are carefully screened and there is a long waiting list in both categories.
Lake Parc is no longer considered a blighting influence on its
surroundings, a change from the days when people in the neighboring communities were agitating to have the project torn down. A
next step planned by the Chicago Housing Authority is to build 564
units of scatter-site, low-rise housing in the neighborhood, with a

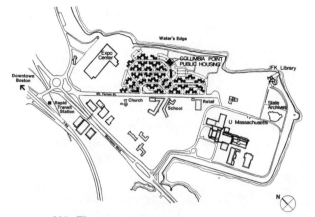

113. The original site plan.

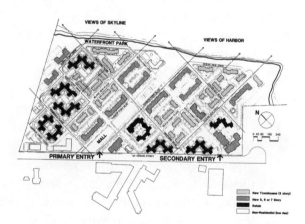

114. The new site plan, by Goody, Clancy & Associates.

quarter of the apartments reserved as replacement housing for the units at Lake Parc that are no longer available to low-income tenants.

Chicago's Leadership Council for Metropolitan Communities is a private organization largely financed by government grants that has helped 5,600 families move from inner-city public housing to houses and apartments in other neighborhoods, using federal housing funds that pay the difference between the rent charged by a private landlord and the rent the tenant can afford to pay, calculated as one fourth the tenant's gross income. This dispersal program was begun in the late 1970s in response to legal requirements that

Chicago stop concentrating public housing tenants in a few inner-city locations.

While these Chicago programs have been too small to have a major effect on the city, they seem to frame a policy that could be extended in Chicago and in other cities: help some low-income families to move out of distressed inner-city housing projects, then convert the projects to mixed-income communities, so that the low-income tenants who remain are living in a different social environment.

Other cities, including Norfolk and Dallas, are investigating ways to turn housing projects into communities. In Dallas, Steven Peterson and Barbara Littenberg have demonstrated ways in which Lake West, a 3,500-unit low-income project, can be turned into a true urban neighborhood. Their master plan reorganizes the street system to make links with the adjacent community. Existing housing units, many of them with flat roofs, are to be remodeled with pitched roofs and added detailing to look more like suburban houses. So far, 900 units in this project have been renovated.

In Norfolk, UDA Architects has redesigned the Diggstown Housing project to make it an urban neighborhood. Built as rows of barrackslike buildings in the days when housing project residents were not allowed to own cars [115], a new system of streets has been put through so that most residents can have a parking space right in front of their apartment. Diggstown's buildings have been remodeled to give them new windows, ornamental shutters and large, elegantly detailed front porches. Yards have been divided, fenced, and provided with a backyard storage shed for each apartment [116]. Gates in the fences for individual yards can be opened only by the house key for the unit the yard belongs to, and new landscaping and powerful new outdoor lighting are also part of the redesign. Crime and vandalism are expected to go down now that residents can control their own environment and take pride in their immediate surroundings, and the quality of life should go way up [117].

Private housing in bypassed neighborhoods has become the housing of last resort, and conditions in these buildings often do not meet the building code. Slum conditions in every city are illegal, but public officials are often reluctant to force compliance with

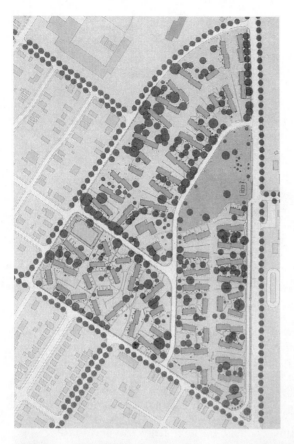

115. *At top, an axonometric plan of Norfolk's Diggstown Housing, buildings set amid open space that belongs to no one and is isolated from streets, reflecting partly the design ideology of Modernism, and partly that residents were not permitted to own cars.*

116. *Partial view of the renovations showing new streets and fenced-in private yards.*

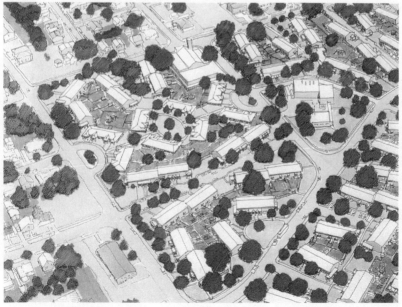

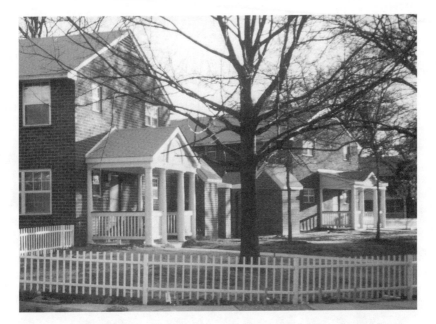

117. New porches and window details make buildings look like suburban houses or garden apartments, rather than barracks—a home, rather than a holding area. The redesign is by UDA Architects.

codes, because they are afraid the landlord will then abandon the building, and the city will not have the money either to operate the building or to correct the code violations. Strictly enforced compliance, unsupported by funds for repairs, can end up evicting tenants to permit the demolition of the building, and thus the creation of more homelessness. However, public policy should not permit a substantial fraction of every city's housing to be operated in violation of the basic standards in the building code. This is as much an emergency as the aftermath of a hurricane, although the disaster has happened in slow motion. It is a situation, like school desegregation, where the courts could be used to compel the executive branch to take action; but the best use of the courts would be for responsible officials to prosecute building owners who persist in breaking the law.

Cities know that the money they are paying out as welfare is often used for rent in buildings that do not come close to meeting the code. There ought to be some way that the rent paid by welfare recipients could be used as leverage to ensure that their housing meets minimum standards. Computerized databases ought to be able to pinpoint buildings where public money is subsidizing illegal conditions.

Renovation of existing buildings is usually less expensive than new construction; loan funds are needed to help responsible private owners renovate buildings before deterioration makes demolition or complete reconstruction the only alternatives.

There is a long history of lenders discriminating against members of minority groups and against inner-city locations. There are now laws against such discrimination and more investment in old-city residential areas, although changed lending policies and mortgage guarantees from government agencies are not always enough, particularly when a whole neighborhood is badly deteriorated. Substandard housing owned by absentee landlords remains the biggest problem.

Many of the worst urban neighborhoods are in excellent locations, close to city centers, with a complete infrastructure system already in place. There is a tremendous amount of underused land in these neighborhoods. As noted in the previous chapter, at some point these inner-city locations become competitive with locations on the urban fringe that have no existing infrastructure and are a long commute away from employment centers. Encouraging higher-income people to live in these areas can help low-income people also. When only the lowest-income groups live in an area, many community institutions (like Boy Scouts, Girl Scouts, women's clubs, lodges) disappear. Creating a community requires mixing incomes, in private buildings just as in public housing.

The large amount of available land in inner-city neighborhoods raises the possibility of self-help housing. Habitat for Humanity and other groups have demonstrated that it is possible to build good housing in inner-city neighborhoods, with the participation of volunteers and the future tenants, for less than costs of similar buildings produced by the housing industry. So far, cities have not been using these efforts to plan for the incremental transformation of whole neighborhoods.

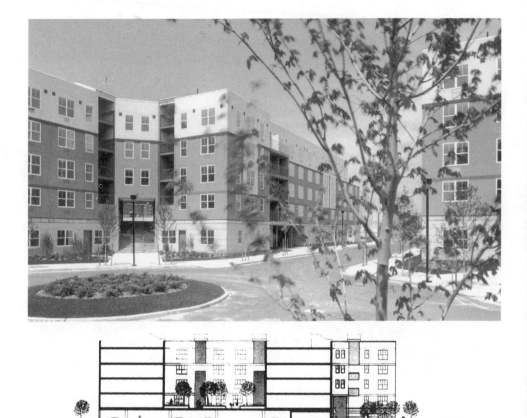

118. *Spring Creek houses showing entrance stairs to private courtyard above the parking.*

119. *Section shows how parking is placed under the buildings, permitting urban blocks rather than alternating houses and parking lots. The Liebman/Melting Partnership are the architects.*

Another housing prototype that could be used in many inner-city neighborhoods is the Spring Creek housing in south Brooklyn, designed by the Liebman/Melting partnership [118]. Parking at ground level is covered by a landscaped deck, which becomes a safe, controlled access area for town houses and apartments. The deck is accessible from a flight of stairs and an elevator for the elderly or handicapped [119]. The street side of the parking area is lined with ground-floor apartments or professional offices.

Another prototype is the single-room apartment hotel. Cities were too quick to discard this building type by zoning it out of existence or letting it be replaced by other development. Many single-room buildings were substandard and run-down, but a small, well-maintained room with plumbing and minimal kitchen equipment can be perfectly acceptable housing. It is certainly superior to being homeless. San Francisco and San Diego are two cities that have recently been building new single-room occupancy hotels. The plans for residence hotel rooms in San Diego, designed by architect Rob Wellington Quigley [120, 121], show that living in a very small space does not have to be a dreary, dead-end experience.

A third alternative low-income housing type, the boarding house, has almost disappeared from cities (in many cases because of zoning), although its up-scale analogue, the bed-and-breakfast hotel, continues to thrive. Again, there was a potential for such buildings to be run exploitively, but, at their best, they met the needs of a large number of people who could not afford apartments of their own. Recent interest in cohousing and other forms of group living may represent a rebirth of inexpensive congregate living in cities.

Neighborhoods with decent, affordable housing still need good schools if they are to attract people who have a choice about where they live. Jonathan Kozol's latest report on the public schools, *Savage Inequalities*, makes it clear that what is wrong with most inner-city education is that it is still segregated, separate, and unequal. Money is the basic problem, not governance or curriculum.

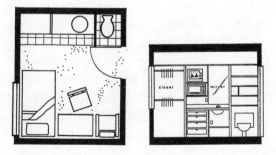

120, 121. Plan and interior elevation of a room in a single-room hotel designed by Rob Wellington Quigley. Small, low-cost accommodation does not need to be squalid.

Recent court decisions have unlocked funds for the Kansas City, Missouri, school district, which may provide a demonstration of what can happen in an urban school system if it receives a level of support equivalent to that possible in a relatively affluent suburb.

The Harriet Tubman Elementary School in Newark, New Jersey, has been described as an "island of excellence" in an otherwise severely troubled inner-city school district. The difference comes from the determination of the school's principal, who has pushed for high educational standards, has involved the parents of the children in her efforts, and has successfully obtained the additional funding needed from foundations. An additional $50,000 a year has been enough to make a decisive improvement, by providing books and equipment that the school district could not supply, financing after-school programs for "latch-key" children, and paying for special teacher-training courses. Why is the exception not the norm?

Cities have to maintain a social infrastructure and social safety net for all areas, but with social services funded from the local tax base, often there is not enough money to go around. Poor neighborhoods need the most services, but these districts usually have less political influence, and thus less governmental support, than other areas. No one with any ability to choose is going to live in a neighborhood that has obviously been written off by the city administration.

Removing physical causes of urban blight can also make a difference in poor neighborhoods, which generally have a high concentration of railway tracks, power lines, and highway viaducts. When highways run through affluent communities, noise reduction measures, such as fences and berms, are routinely introduced to cut down on noise pollution. The same is seldom done for poor areas. When electrical substations are required in affluent communities, the substations are enclosed and made to look like buildings; in poor neighborhoods the transformers are out in the open. Many of these neighborhoods originally lost real estate value because of elevated railway lines, highway viaducts, power easements, or other blighting influences. Until highways and utilities in bypassed urban neighborhoods are given the same treatment that richer neighborhoods routinely receive, investment in these bypassed areas will always be questionable.

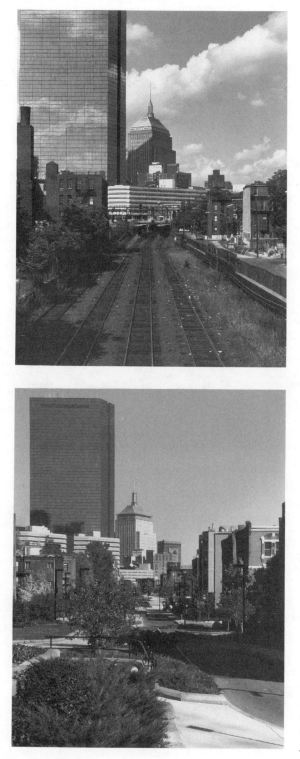

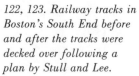

122, 123. Railway tracks in Boston's South End before and after the tracks were decked over following a plan by Stull and Lee.

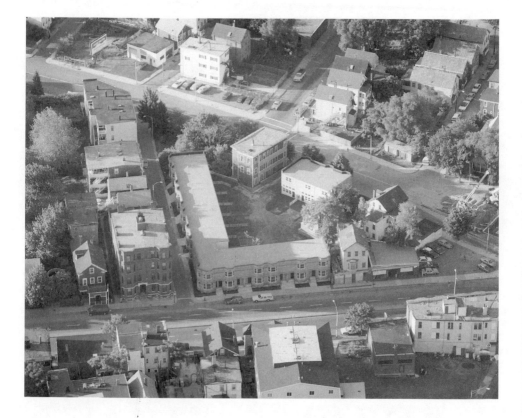

One of the most spectacular examples of removing a blighting
influence is the rebuilding of Boston's Central Artery as a tunnel
instead of an elevated highway, as described in chapter 6. A less
costly, but still impressive initiative has been the improvements to
Boston's southwest rail corridor, including the decking of the main-
line tracks as they go through Boston's South End and Back Bay
districts [122, 123], which has greatly improved a badly deteriorated area. Such investments are needed in the low-income districts of every city: to finance buffers along highways, the shielding
of power lines, and the restoration of derelict land as park, as along
the Mystic River in metropolitan Boston.

Fifty years of Cold War conditions have made public-works funding
at this scale almost unimaginable. Now that the U.S. is returning to
a peacetime economy, it should be possible to make plans for this
kind of investment in cities, particularly as removing blighting
influences will raise values of nearby property. There is also still a

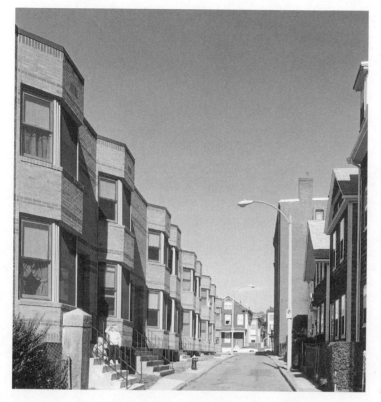

124, 125. Low-cost housing developed by the Bricklayers Union, fitted into a small site in a Boston neighborhood. The architects are William Rawn and Associates.

place for traditional urban renewal techniques in blighted areas, particularly in places where buildings and blocks are largely deserted and there need be little or no relocation. Land does not need to be written down, but often the public sector can create development parcels by condemnation when land has too fragmented an ownership to be assembled privately.

The future of older cities depends ultimately on public policy initiatives that they cannot control directly. Older centers and neighborhoods need rapid-transit links to the new centers in formerly suburban areas so that the metropolitan area can function as one economy and not split into two. Metropolitan services have to be supported by an equalized tax base; there need to be limits to growth at the metropolitan fringe accompanied by major new investment in bypassed residential neighborhoods and derelict industrial districts. Reintegrating the metropolitan area is necessary for the survival of cities, suburbs, and the regional eco-system.

Part III
Reshaping
the Metropolitan Region

9

The Changing Philosophy of Planning and Design

"Let the market decide," runs a well-rehearsed argument against urban and regional planning. "Government interference only makes matters worse."

The difficulty with this assertion is that zoning and building codes, environmental regulations, tax incentives, and public transportation subsidies are all an integral part of today's complex real estate market. The real opposition is not between regulation and no regulation, or incentives and no incentives, but between a real estate market affected by a series of unrelated government actions or an environment for real estate investment created by planned and coordinated government actions. Regulation and incentives already shape private development; if the public is getting what it asks for, why shouldn't it ask for something better?

The expansion of government intervention that began with highways, subsidized housing, and urban renewal has grown to include complex objectives such as environmental protection, social welfare, and economic development. The limited definition of planning that was adopted when implementation was restricted to development regulations and public-works projects clearly has had to change to accommodate these new public purposes.

One of the most important changes has been the addition of design methods to the practice of planning. Design is a way of making complex decisions where a series of potential actions are interrelated and choices on one issue affect choices about others. Such decisions are made routinely in the design of houses and more complex buildings, in engineering, and in landscape architecture.

Design methodology applied to public policy means understanding, and planning, the interactions between a highway and surrounding neighborhoods; it means understanding that zoning regulations inevitably shape buildings and that these design consequences should be anticipated and intended. Subdivision of land into lots and streets is not just a way of offering parcels for sale, but shapes a new neighborhood. Building public housing is not just a way of eradicating slums or moving people out of substandard quarters, but creates new communities. Urban renewal in city centers is not just the removal of blighted buildings and unproductive ownership patterns, but a strategy for reorganizing the downtown. Over the last generation there has been growing recognition that planning decisions often carry a large design component, and that skilled city designers are needed to help make these decisions and carry them out. There is still resistance to urban design by those who argue that design decisions are not objective, and that government has no business making them. But if government continues to intervene in development as it has been doing, it is inevitably making important design decisions about the future of cities and towns. Making decisions blindly does not exonerate government from responsibility for the results.

Another major change in planning method is community participation in planning, which is also a direct consequence of today's larger scale of public intervention in the development of cities and towns. When government's role was confined to regulations and public works, it was easier for officials to make decisions on behalf of the public, as there were already shared assumptions about objectives and methods. As public intervention increased, decisions inevitably affected more people and became more controversial. It is now axiomatic that any major public action requires ample advance notice and review, and the public is now involved in shaping many of these decisions while they are being made.

Designers are used to working with clients, sketching out alternative hypotheses, evaluating them, synthesizing new possibilities from the discussion. The addition to the planning profession of people trained in design has aided the acceptance of public participation and made it more effective. Of course, even when a wide range of people have had ample time to participate in a plan, it does not mean that they all will be satisfied. Even the design of a house can lead to serious tensions between architect and client.

The emergence of what might be called design consumerism, an interest in the way the public actually uses and experiences public buildings and public spaces, has been another consequence of both increased public intervention and community participation in city planning and design. When the developer of an office building receives a bonus of additional floor area for providing a public plaza, the design is an important means of making sure the plaza serves a public purpose. The design of many privately built public spaces in big cities deliberately discouraged anyone from using them. Public standards for seating space, sunlight, and landscaping help ensure that these spaces attract people and activities.

The conservation ethic and the concept of sustainability represent another major change in planning philosophy: people should manage the environment so that it can sustain future generations, and not just themselves. Sustainability requires matching development intensity to the carrying capacity of the land—the concept behind the environmental zoning discussed in chapter 3—plus many other public policies to conserve non-renewable resources as much as possible. Ecologists have discovered that the environment itself is the equivalent of a design that has evolved over a long period of time, through the complex interactions of many different factors. A kind of reverse engineering or reverse design is used to decode the origins of the current environment. Constant incremental change is a normal part of the environment, but the complexity of environmental interactions suggests that it is best to avoid major interventions, unless there can be complete confidence that what is being proposed is an improvement, and will interact positively with existing conditions.

Environmental conservatism also leads to a policy of preserving old buildings, not just because they may be of historic or architectural interest, but because they represent a commitment of natural resources. Generations of public officials have been encouraged to demolish buildings because they were impediments to a future "highest and best use" of the land. The conservation ethic suggests the opposite policy: old buildings have value. They were bought and paid for long ago; their materials and the energy needed to replace them are better conserved.

As designers have become more involved in urban and regional problems, they have responded to criticism by environmentalists and historic preservationists by paying more attention to the context of their work, and by creating buildings and landscapes that emulate the virtues of established areas, and are more compatible with nearby buildings, environments, or historic districts.

Designers have also learned that while a building, a bridge, or a park is a clearly defined product with a form that will remain fixed for a long time, city designs cannot be fixed in the same way. Architects and landscape architects have had to modify their belief that cities or towns could be completed in a single image. The pace of social and technological change is too rapid, the variety of public requirements is too great, and there is no single design philosophy that is valid in all situations.

Up until the early 1930s it was possible to believe that all the components of a designed city had been invented, and that in time every city could be perfected. Downtown would have its civic center in the academic classical style made popular by the Chicago Exposition of 1893. The tall buildings of the office district could be reorganized so that they too were arranged around a civic mall, like the buildings along Park Avenue north of Grand Central Station in New York, or Rockefeller Center, or the Terminal Tower complex on the southeast corner of Cleveland's Public Square. The central city would be set in a park and boulevard system like the one created along the Chicago lakefront. While factories would remain strictly utilitarian, dreary or deteriorating working-class neighborhoods could be gradually converted to garden districts, like Sunnyside Gardens in New York City. Slums could be cleared and replaced with groups of apartment buildings around landscaped courtyards, like some of the prototypes constructed by the Phipps Foundation, also in New York City. Parkways and boulevards would lead to garden suburbs like River Oaks or Palos Verdes. By the 1930s the fashionable residential districts of most American cities were already garden suburbs, and there were also some new prototypes for suburban downtowns: the centers of Shaker Heights and Lake Forest, the Country Club shopping center in Kansas City.

The first Regional Plan for New York City, published in 1929, put forward these ingredients of the designed city with the conviction that they were a comprehensive prescription for the future. Over the next decade the vision set down by the confident planners of the late 1920s was codified in zoning and subdivision ordinances, highway designs, and government housing standards.

Since the 1929 Regional Plan the metropolis has changed almost out of recognition, and the theory of design has changed also. The 1930s saw the introduction into the United States of the modernist doctrine in architecture. Its practitioners advocated stripping away the classical trappings that had adorned public buildings and the references to Tudor, Spanish, or Colonial design that had satisfied the pretensions of suburban homeowners. Modernist architects, reacting against insanitary nineteenth-century lightwells and courtyards, also advocated freeing buildings from the old urban street system and surrounding buildings with open space: towers in a park.

This intellectual housecleaning also got rid of the principles of city and town design that had been accepted without question by generations of architects and planners: the idea of coherent outdoor spaces, the importance of architectural continuity along streets, the significance of vistas. Modernism created a new vocabulary for buildings, but no equivalent rationale for city design. Surrounding buildings with open space did not work well in existing cities where redevelopment was incremental and the resulting spaces fragmentary. The tower in the park worked even less well in new developments, because the separation of buildings made it difficult for people to walk from one destination to another. The doctrine of the tower in a park led inexorably to the reality of the tower in a parking lot.

When the great suburban expansion took place after World War II, rules based on prewar practice governed new development. But standards derived from garden-suburb concepts of the 1920s did not work as well when they were separated from their underpinning of traditional city design ideas. Endless replication of winding streets according to government standards meant nothing without town squares, coherent relationships of buildings to streets, and planned vistas and greenways. And of course, suburban zoning and street standards had never been conceived as a setting for tall buildings, or for regional shopping centers and office parks.

The lack of traditional city design ideas was at first seen as an advantage. Planners decided that they had been freed from pretentious and elitist notions that had no current social relevance.

In the cities, many older areas were cleared by government-supported urban renewal, both for housing and for downtown redevelopment. These renewal policies should have created great opportunities for a better city, but the new buildings followed modernist architectural doctrine. Each building was planned as a separate project, designed from the inside out, with little reference to its neighbors. Post–World War II urban renewal produced few city designs as good as Rockefeller Center or Tower City. The best of the renewal areas, like Southwest Washington or Constitution Plaza in Hartford, have an abstract elegance of composition but are deliberately detached from the life of the surrounding city.

Doctrines of modernist architectural austerity reinforced the natural inclination of governments not to spend money where expenditures could not be clearly justified. During almost the whole of the post–World War II period, the U.S. remained in what amounted to a war economy, which after several decades came to seem a normal condition. Building costs were higher and budgets lower than during the prosperous peacetime era before 1929.

Government buildings not only were stripped of domes and colonnades, but no longer were arranged to create civic spaces. The Interstate highway system was built with no extra land for the landscaped buffer zones that had characterized prewar parkway design, only minimal expenditures for plantings within the right-of-way, and no attempt to design bridges and roadside buildings with the kinds of civic design elements that were routine in the 1920s. When the new highways were built through populated areas, they were constructed with an indifference to their surroundings that repeated the worst mistakes made during the development of the railroads. Publicly supported housing lost any sense of humane scale, as projects were made denser and denser to create ever more efficient ratios of apartments to land cost.

By the 1960s it was becoming evident that something was drastically wrong with city development in the United States, and that urban design considerations were not as irrelevant as planners and government officials had thought. A new generation of designers began looking at city design problems. I have described part of this process in two previous books: *Urban Design as Public Policy* and *Introduction to Urban Design*.

The modernist revolution in architecture had been needed because of innovations in technology: steel and concrete frames, elevators, artificial light, air conditioning, walls of glass. In the same way cities changed because of new forms of transportation and the potential of a good life for almost everyone.

But the great pioneers of modern architecture, like Le Corbusier and Walter Gropius, assumed that cities could be perfected in a new image; for them the past had only sentimental value. They also assumed that the collective life of society was far more important than the interests of individuals. They have been proved wrong. Aldo Rossi has written eloquently in *The Architecture of the City* of the renewed understanding that cities reflect the aspirations of many different interests, and are perceived through a series of individual recollections in which the experience of other cities, of the past, and even of unbuilt city designs all play a part.

At the same time, designing a city is not like making a painting or a sculpture, it is not an expression of individual will or private sensibility. Colin Rowe and Fred Koetter argued in *Collage City* that the designer should intervene in the existing city by adding to and adjusting what is already there, a process more like collage than any other art form.

Design of built-up areas begins with what already exists, just as design in unbuilt areas begins with the natural landscape. Modernist architectural doctrine gave an intellectual license to the extensive demolition of valuable old buildings in the 1950s and 1960s. Preservationists reacted with justifiable outrage, which drew part of its energy from disgust with the design of most new buildings and their effect on the city. The preservation movement helped create a constituency for better city design.

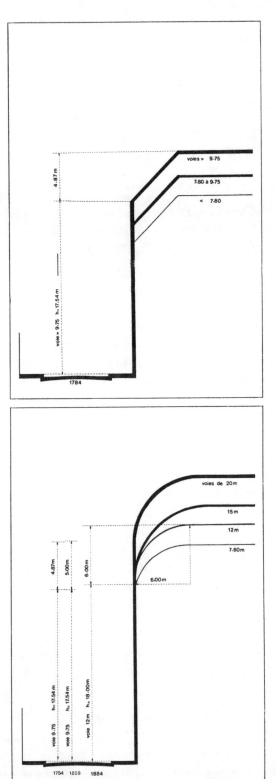

126. *Historian Norma Evenson catalogued four stages in the evolution of Parisian development controls. Building height was related to street width; the setback angle in the regulations helped create the distinctive Parisian roofscape.*

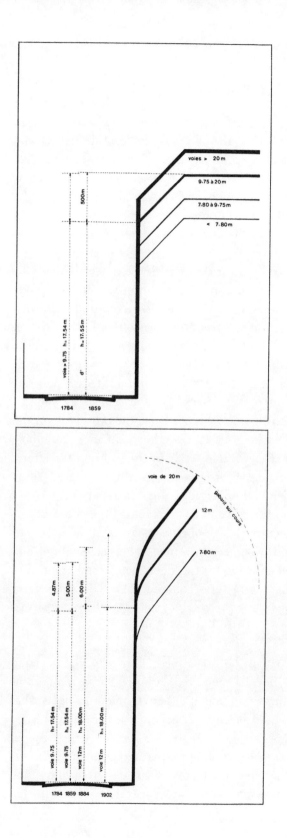

While architects had been arguing about style and drawing utopian cities that would all be designed in a single image, all the real design decisions about cities were being made by the engineers who laid out streets and infrastructure, the planners and legal specialists who wrote the development regulations, the entrepreneurs who promoted new buildings, and the public officials who authorized new government expenditures. Anyone who wanted to influence the design of cities needed to learn to influence the incremental process by which city development decisions are actually made.

Designers had to discover how to rewrite development regulations to ensure that appropriate design relationships are achieved. They took another look at some of the most successful examples of urban design, such as the creation of Paris, and learned that Paris has been imposing design guidelines for more than two centuries. From 1784 onward, Parisian legislation related building height to street widths and imposed a setback angle for attics. In addition, facade controls could be adopted for important streets. The Parisian street-wall and attic control as seen in Illustration 126 became the prototype for the bulk control in New York City's 1916 zoning ordinance. Buildings could rise to a height that was a function of the width of the street, as in Paris, and then had to set back beneath an angled "sky-exposure plane," which is the Parisian attic translated to the larger scale of the elevator building [127]. Understanding the power of this one simple idea to affect the design of cities as disparate as Paris and New York encouraged designers to return to the elements of city design that were pushed aside by the doctrine of modernism but that turn out to be necessary for a coherent city. This time, however, these concepts were expressed as relatively abstract, formal guidelines as stylistically neutral as possible.

If design relationships can be objectified, they can be translated relatively easily into development regulations. These regulations inform private investors and planners of government projects what the public interest should be in each part of the central area.

The most important consideration in preparing design guidelines is that they be put on the table in advance of the design of individual projects, so that investors and the architect are on notice about what

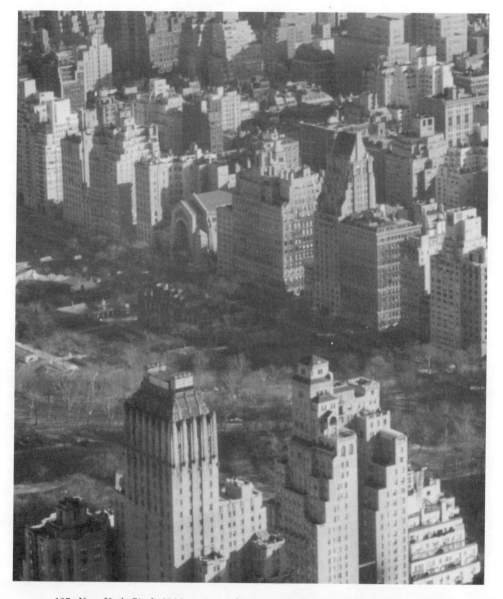

127. New York City's 1916 zoning ordinance took the concept of relating setbacks above a certain height to street width and enlarged the scale to regulate the elevator building. Instead of the Parisian garret, the New York controls create an architecture of setbacks and terraces.

is expected and have time to assimilate them into the list of factors that determine the design.

Guidelines do limit the options before investors and designers, but so do many other factors. Adding a building to a city or a landscape requires a complex series of choices; and the public interest requires that each building play a constructive part in the evolution of each area. What city designers have learned to do is to create the framework within which growth and change can occur. Current projects can be designed in detail; developments expected in 10 years can be sketched out; the more distant future can be anticipated, but the possibility of change must be built into the design.

10

The Elements of City Design

ccepting that the design of all human settlements begins by
understanding the natural landscape means changing many
standard planning and design procedures. Plans for building in rural, undeveloped areas should start with a regional geographic analysis that maps streams, steep hillsides, wetlands, patterns of vegetation, and subsoil conditions. The carrying capacity of
the natural environment becomes a basis for locating transportation
systems, settlements, and growth boundaries. Development regulations like zoning and subdivision ordinances are modified to include
carrying capacity as a basis for density calculations, as discussed in
chapter 3.

Regional planning thus becomes a design problem in which understanding both natural systems and the functional organization of
existing development helps locate transportation systems, commercial centers, and growth boundaries. As noted in chapter 4, local
governments are not accustomed to making affirmative decisions
about which areas of the natural landscape ought to be preserved
and which areas should be built up. For example, it is easier to
designate a development corridor for the full length of a highway
than to pick locations for commercial centers, but choosing locations is what needs to be done. For the designer, as opposed to the
politician, these kinds of decisions can be relatively easy. The places
with the best combination of access and land suitable for building
are the locations that should be designated, as shown in Illustration 33.

In cities or suburban locations where development has already
taken place, the existing streets, parks, and buildings set the context
for new construction. While demolition and change are often necessary, the appropriate design response is always conditioned by
specific circumstances. Rather than applying an abstract, preexist-

ing set of ideas, successful city design becomes situational, seeking a new pattern in response to existing geography, buildings, and the uncompleted design intentions of previous developments.

In a previous book, *The Elusive City*, I have outlined four different concepts of city and regional design: the monumental city, derived from classical and Renaissance architecture; the garden city or suburb shaped originally by English landscape design and the picturesque aesthetic; the modernist city; and the city as a megastructure. Component parts of existing cities have been built in accordance with each of these design approaches, and each continues to be used in new development. The city designer may have an individual preference, but it is necessary to understand the significance of each design alternative. Each implies different ways of responding to nature and creates different internal organizations in plan and in three dimensions.

Monumental city design is based on an axis of symmetry and a hierarchy of parts controlled from a central point. Washington, D.C., is a good example of a monumental city plan: the axis of the Capitol is extended westward to form the Mall, and the axis of the White House extends north up Sixteenth Street and south to the Jefferson Memorial. The central point is the meeting of the two axes, which Major L'Enfant, the original designer, designated as the site of the Washington Monument. Many civic centers and state capitol groups are designed according to these monumental principles.

The reservation of Rock Creek Park brought the English landscape aesthetic into Washington as a counterpoint to its monumental street plan, and Washington's early garden suburbs, like Chevy Chase, are related to this park. Most American cities have at least one upper-income garden suburb built during the early years of this century, with tree-lined, winding streets and generous parks and greenways.

Modernist city design recognized that providing light and views to all sides of a tall building meant more separation among towers than was traditional with lower structures. In addition, the automobile implied a fundamental change in city organization: arterial streets and expressways permitted almost continuous development, and tall buildings could occur anywhere, not just in the old urban centers. Modernist city design has produced the familiar pattern of isolated elements strung out along the highway. Urban spaces in modernist design are separated from the street, cleared of pre-existing buildings and vegetation and defined by buildings organized in abstract patterns, almost always deliberately asymmetrical.

The megastructure concept of city design was in part an avant-garde idea of the 1960s. Paolo Soleri's studies for "arcologies" containing millions of people are drawings of megastructures. The idea that cities could become enormous buildings seems to be a logical extension of the closely packed but separate structures of a city center, connected by streets and supported by complex utility systems buried underground. Why not design the whole thing more efficiently, make the utilities and the public spaces part of the building and control their access and climate? This is the thinking that lies behind Buckminster Fuller's photomontage of a giant geodesic dome covering most of Midtown and Lower Manhattan. The technical, financial, and social problems implicit in such an idea are mind-boggling, but many downtown mixed-use centers, suburban shopping malls, and airports are megastructures at a smaller scale.

Three basic components of any city design are the organization of public open space—including streets, plazas, and parks or gardens—the architectural relationships among buildings, and the composition of building mass in relation to the landscape or the skyline. The potential organization and shape of each of these urban components can differ, depending on the city design concept adopted.

In monumental city design the street is usually straight; if curved, it is part of some geometric figure. Buildings are used to reinforce and define the space of the street, or of squares and open spaces. In a garden suburb the street is usually curved and is designed as a parkway dominated by trees, lawns, and clusters of shrubbery. Buildings are incidents in a continuous landscape. Modernist design detaches the street from both buildings and landscape. In the megastructure, the street is internalized; it becomes a climate-controlled mall.

In monumental city design, urban space is surrounded and defined by buildings, or is organized by architectural concepts, like the axis, that extend into the landscape. In the picturesque garden tradition, exterior spaces are designed naturalistically to appear as if they have always been part of the landscape. Modernist urban space is often a setting for buildings, rather than a place enclosed by buildings: space and architecture form an abstract composition. In a mega-structure, the space is brought indoors, enclosed as atriums or concourses and made part of the building.

In monumental city design, groups of buildings have their own inner logic, usually symmetrical, and are sited to dominate the landscape. The picturesque designs that are part of the garden-suburb tradition compose buildings asymmetrically and site them to blend in with the landscape. Modernist building masses are usually asymmetrical and sited in juxtaposition to the natural land-scape, while the megastructure is based on repeating elements that tend to bring the natural landscape within the megastructural system.

As described in chapter 5, the geography of cities evolved over time into functional commercial or manufacturing districts and residen-tial precincts. In preindustrial times, residential precincts tended to be centered around the palatial house of an important clan leader or the precinct was the parish of a religious building. The concept that cities should have neighborhoods was put forward as a way of giving a comparable structure to the residential areas of a modern city.

The fourth meeting of the Congrès Internationaux d'Architecture Moderne (C.I.A.M.) adopted the theory of the neighborhood, as put forward by Clarence Perry, but without Perry's garden-suburb con-figuration, shown in Illustration 47. The residential districts in Brasilia, a completed example of the kind of city advocated by C.I.A.M., are organized along a central highway. At each exit from the highway, a street lined with shops serves four surrounding residential quadrants of apartment buildings. Beyond the apart-ment houses are lower-density tracts of single-family houses. Most of the apartments are within walking distance of the shops, but lower-density housing is farther away from shops and services.

Rigid segregation of building types means that subareas tend to group people with similar incomes. Brasilia's neighborhoods and streets are all known by the numbers which place them in the overall grid. The plan is as rationalist as possible; the planners shunned the romantic atmosphere of the garden suburb visible in Clarence Perry's diagram of the neighborhood. The expressway system is the spine of the city and major destinations are widely separated.

In other modern cities, garden-suburb street plans are used, but often only as a module in a larger repeating pattern. The planned community of Irvine, California, has residential neighborhoods laid out like garden suburbs, with winding streets and cul-de-sacs, but the master plan separates each neighborhood from the main streets and from each other, creating separate communities with their own internal street systems, sometimes protected by a gatehouse.

This standard development practice is the object of attack by many designers, as discussed in chapter 4, who feel that all streets in a community should be connected and that neighborhoods should be planned as if they were separate villages. Each such neighborhood would have different-sized houses and apartments and its own center and distinctive institutions. Distances would be walkable, and, if possible, each neighborhood would also have shops and other services.

This critique of the modernist city is heavily dependent on planning texts written before modernism became the dominant style, notably Raymond Unwin's *Town Planning in Practice* and the *Neighborhood and Community Planning* volume of the 1929 Regional Survey and Plan for New York. Designers are also looking again at premodernist plans influenced by monumental design principles, like the many communities designed by John Nolen. The eloquent drawings of Leon Krier, illustrating the urban coherence and order possible in monumental city design, are another significant current influence.

Leon Krier himself is beginning to make designs for real situations, but the drawings in which he established his theoretical positions are of imaginary projects or hypothetical reconstructions. He thus had the luxury of not dealing with innovations that are inconsistent with the monumental tradition. For Krier the automobile is not a mode of transportation but a way to make weekend excursions away from the city; the limited-access highway should never have been invented, and the elevator is for observation towers, not the means of creating tall office buildings, apartments, or hotels.

Krier thus avoids the difficulties of reconciling tall buildings with lower structures, or the need to incorporate parking and highway viaducts within a physical fabric defined by streets and buildings. These are precisely the most difficult and central problems of urban design today. Looking back at early-twentieth-century design solutions will not solve these problems either. Raymond Unwin and Clarence Perry never had to deal with the implications of universal car ownership, or high intensity development in formerly suburban locations.

The modernist designers assumed that towers, highways, and parking lots meant that city design had to take entirely new forms. There are places within the metropolis where a dramatic juxtaposition of tower and highway and the creation of grand expanses of parking lot are appropriate design solutions. Where old cities continue to exist, however, and where new cities need some of the amenities of older development, ways have to be found to assimilate the tower, the highway, and the parking lot into a continuous urban fabric.

The modernist tower, removed from street frontage and set in a park or plaza, has been shown not to work well within intensely developed existing cities, producing irregular breaks in the street frontage and opening up vistas to the undesigned party walls of adjacent buildings. Experience has led city designers to seek to reestablish the primacy of the street in urban settings and go back to a mix of uses in central areas, rather than create the separate tower zones for office buildings that characterized many urban renewal plans.

Legislation that makes these kinds of urban design considerations part of zoning and other development regulations was pioneered during the 1960s in New York City. Later experience has led to sets of guidelines for large urban developments like Battery Park City, and guidelines that apply to whole urban areas.

Cleveland has a set of design guidelines, covering all downtown districts, that confirms the street system as the dominant design element and seeks to incorporate new development into the existing building fabric, most of which was constructed before modernist towers came to downtown Cleveland. These guidelines also define public open spaces, map pedestrian connections, mandate street level retail frontages in appropriate locations, and delineate tower locations [128]. Letting the tower rise directly from the property line at the edge of the street can produce a good design at the right place, such as the tower designed by Cesar Pelli for the block that links Cleveland's Public Square with the Civic Mall [129]. Towers at the building line integrate the tall building with street-level retail uses. As an overall strategy, however, towers set at the building-line produce dark, canyonlike street spaces, such as the conditions in Lower Manhattan that created the demand for New York City's first zoning ordinance in 1916.

In Washington, D.C., where the height limit precludes obtrusive towers, large-scale horizontal buildings have created a different kind of problem. The designers have to do more than just define the street wall with the building, they need to modulate the wall to keep it from becoming monotonous. Washington does not have downtown guidelines that deal with this issue, but a model of what could be required is shown in a building on Franklin Square by Hartman-Cox Architects [130].

The Fifth Avenue side of New York City's Rockefeller Center suggests a conceptual organization for introducing the tall building into the city and for keeping horizontal elements at an appropriate scale: set up a matrix of separate, lower buildings, in scale with, and related to, the surrounding streets, and then set the towers within this matrix. At Rockefeller Center there are four pavilions of similar size and shape, each six stories high, in scale with the dimensions of Fifth Avenue. Each pair of pavilions defines an axis leading to a taller tower set back from the avenue.

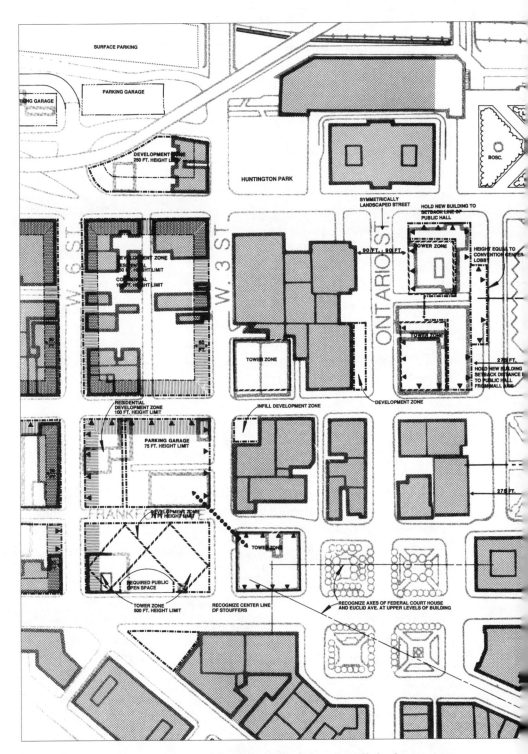

128. *Cleveland now has a set of design guidelines that cover all the downtown districts. In addition to build-to lines along streets, other guidelines define public open space, map pedestrian connections, delineate tower locations, mandate*

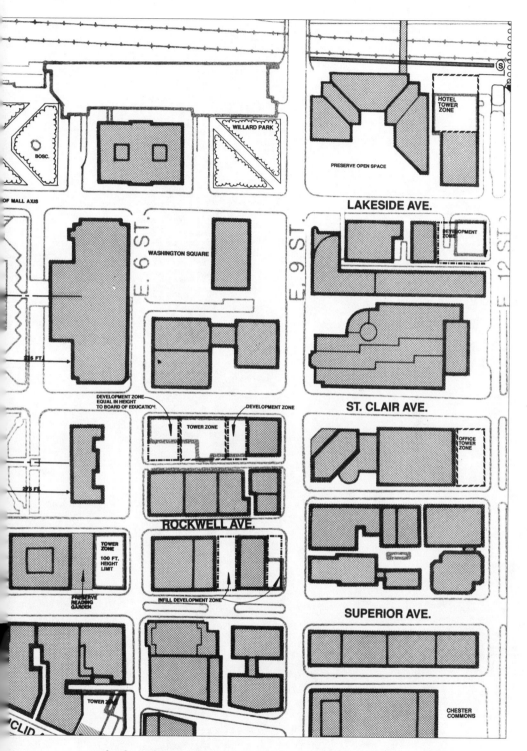

street-level retail space along appropriate frontages, and place service and garage entrances. Plan by the Cleveland City Planning Commission, Jonathan Barnett, consultant.

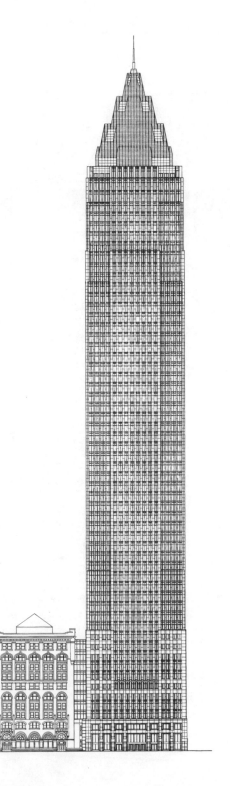

129. The facade of the Society Bank tower by Cesar Pelli has been modulated horizontally to relate to the historic Society Bank building next door, by John Root; the tower has also been modulated vertically, to appear slimmer and to acknowledge its pivotal position between two open spaces.

130. Hartman-Cox Architects have modulated the facade of a building facing Franklin Park in Washington, D.C., to reduce its apparent bulk and to break up what would otherwise be a relentless horizontal mass.

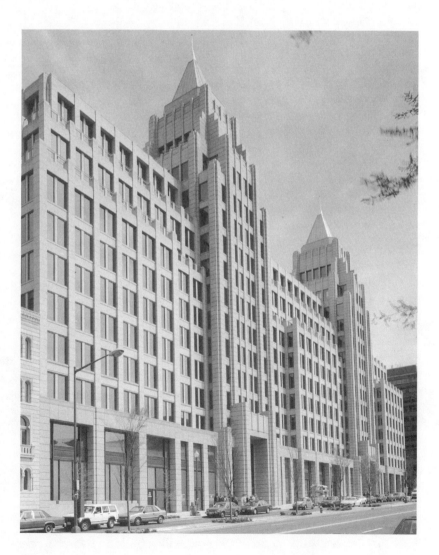

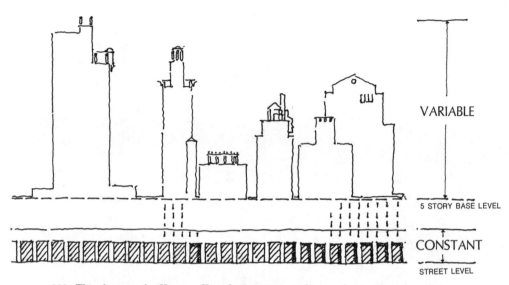

VARIABLE

5 STORY BASE LEVEL

CONSTANT

STREET LEVEL

131. This diagram by Koetter, Kim & Associates indicates that towers of varying sizes and shapes can be placed within a matrix of lower-level buildings that relate to streets.

This conceptual organization is easily translated into design guidelines. It has been used in Cleveland, and in the design guidelines for University Park in Cambridge, Massachusetts, by Koetter, Kim & Associates [131]. It was used in several of New York City's special zoning districts passed in the late 1960s [132], and is the strategy behind a large-scale plan by Cesar Pelli for the Hudson River waterfront across from Manhattan in Weehawken, New Jersey [133].

Guidelines that define the space of the street make use of the build-to line, the opposite of the more familiar setback line. The build-to indication is usually, but not always, set along the edge of the street right-of-way as a direct instruction not to follow the modernist tendency of separating buildings from streets. A specified percentage of the building facade must be constructed along the build-to line. This guideline can ensure that the space of the street or public square continues to be defined.

Holding to a uniform height for the street wall, and setting towers back, is also a useful tactic when new, taller buildings have to be

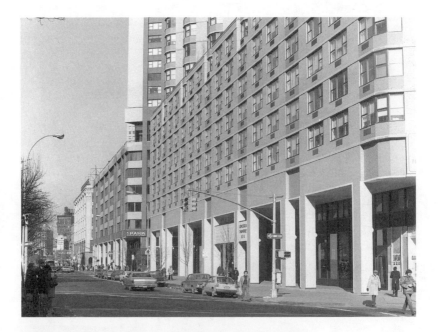

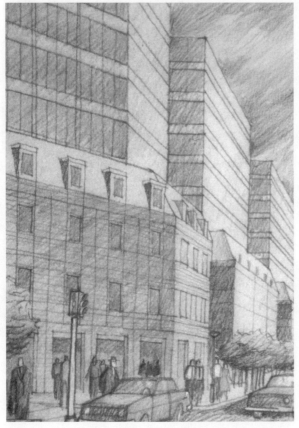

132. New York City's Lincoln Square Special Zoning District required base buildings that held the Broadway facade up to a height of 85 feet, providing a matrix for taller towers.

133. This sketch by Cesar Pelli & Associates shows a concept similar to that of the Lincoln Square District. It is possible for the low buildings to have one character while the towers have a different expression.

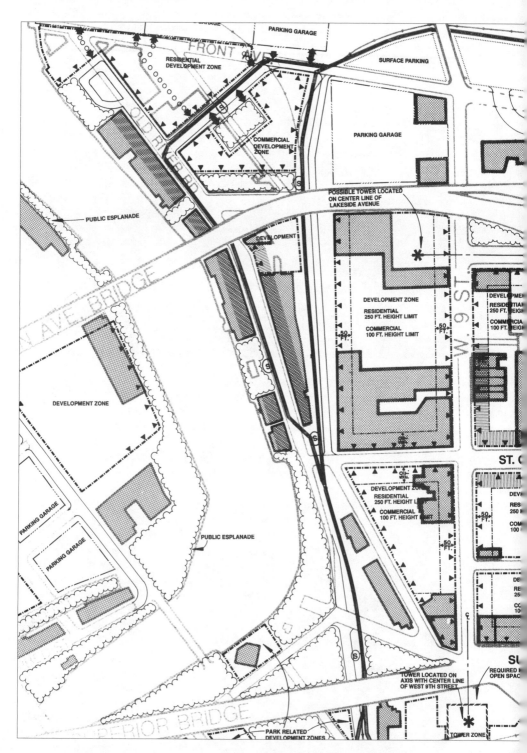

134. The design guidelines for Cleveland's Historic Warehouse District require buildings to hold the street line. The height of the street wall is a function of the prevailing height of existing buildings. Towers must be set back at least 50 feet.

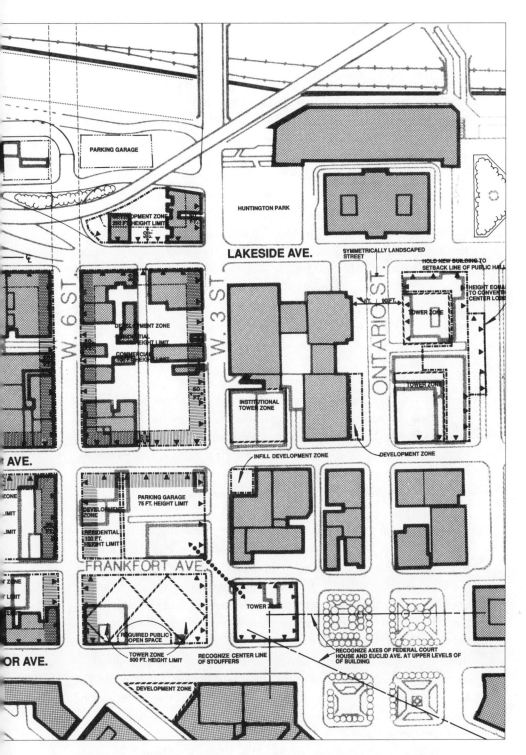

Frontages on designated retail streets must provide shops on the ground floor. Guidelines by the Cleveland City Planning Department, Jonathan Barnett, consultant.

introduced into a historic district. The zoning for the Warehouse District in Cleveland requires developers to hold the street wall to a height determined by the average of existing buildings in the block and set all higher towers back 50 feet. This setback also has the effect of separating the tower from the space of the street, making it seem less intrusive [134].

Having buildings hold the street line also makes it possible for cities to require continuous retail frontages on selected streets. Successful retailing seems to require an uninterrupted sequence of storefronts along a street; if the continuity is broken, business suffers. Guidelines can also require continuity of midblock pedestrian connections, or continuous routes for pedestrian bridges and tunnels.

Entrances and exits for parking and service are important street design issues; if they are located badly they can have a big negative impact on traffic.

In Cleveland the downtown urban design guidelines also identify significant locations where exceptional buildings ought to break free of the building matrix and be designed as towers, such as sites at the end of vistas which need some kind of vertical emphasis. Other significant locations are shown by setback lines to be the place for a required public open space.

Guidelines and regulations can help shape the contributions to the city made by private investors. There are some urban design problems, however, that can only be solved by direct public investment. As discussed in chapter 8, limited-access highways and railway viaducts have had profoundly destructive side effects in cities, fragmenting and blighting neighborhoods and districts at the same time that they help the growth of industry and commercial centers. One design solution, putting railways and highways underground, is obviously very expensive, but the increased property values can pay off in downtown locations. The classic example is the underground railway tunnel that runs from Grand Central Station in New York City northward along elegant and expensive Park Avenue. When the railway emerges at Ninety-Seventh Street and becomes an elevated line on a stone-and-steel trestle, there is an immediate and drastic drop-off in property values. Decking the railway line in

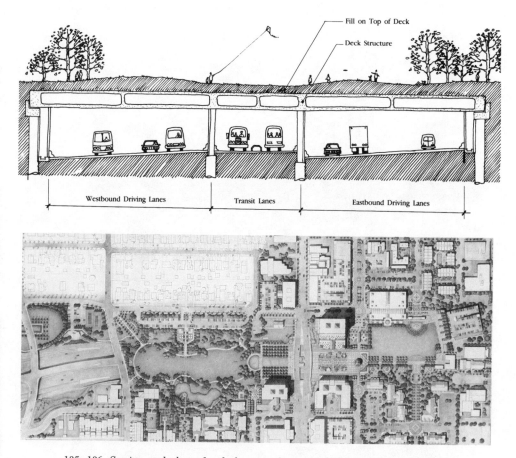

Fill on Top of Deck

Deck Structure

| Westbound Driving Lanes | Transit Lanes | Eastbound Driving Lanes |

135, 136. Section and plan of a deck over a freeway in Phoenix, Arizona, that prevents an important part of the city from being split apart by the highway. The urban designers are HNTB.

Boston's Back Bay district has had a strong effect on restoring the area. Freeway Park in Seattle is an example of a deck introduced over an expressway to help bridge the gap the highway created in the fabric of the city. A more recent instance is the deck over the freeway at Central Avenue in Phoenix [135, 136].

Where viaducts cannot be buried or decked, the best design solutions keep development away from the highway or railway and treat viaducts as if they were natural formations, analogous to rivers or ridge lines, with landscaped buffer zones along each side. Where the highway must be introduced into the midst of a city center or urban neighborhood, the better solution seems to be to drop the highway

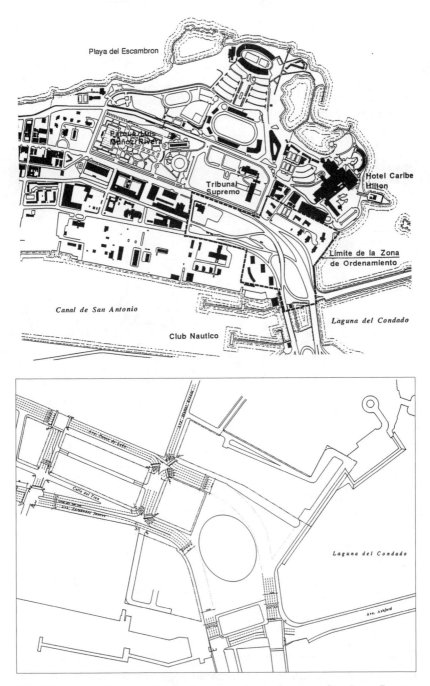

137, 138. A map of an existing grade-separated interchange in San Juan, Puerto Rico, and the design by Koetter, Kim & Associates for replacing the interchange with a boulevard. The new design reduces speed and requires traffic signals, but is far more appropriate in an urban setting.

to grade and treat it as a wide urban boulevard, with traffic at cross streets controlled by traffic signals, as in the rebuilding of New York's formerly elevated West Side Highway. Another example is the design by Koetter, Kim Associates for an important intersection in San Juan, Puerto Rico. The grade-separated highway ramps are to be replaced by a wide boulevard that accommodates all necessary traffic movements [137, 138]. What is lost in speed through such a highway segment is made up for in land values and convenience within the city center.

The introduction of parking lots into downtowns has had a disastrous effect on cities as places, breaking the continuity of building facades and opening out the space of the street in random ways. While it may never be possible to replace all parking lots with garages, it should be possible to zone the most important downtown street frontages for minimum development, so that at least a narrow one-story building is constructed along the street side of parking lots.

The continuous-ramp parking garage, while it is an efficient structure, has a way of looking as if it were a melted building. These appearance problems can be dealt with if they are recognized, for example by keeping the sloping portion of the parking-garage floor away from the street frontage. This strategy is part of an approach to garage design that makes parking structures look like buildings in a city, not segments of a highway that have come to rest on an urban site. Parking garages, being essentially storage, can have a deadening effect on a downtown district. To maintain a continuity of life along the street, ground floors of parking structures can be designed to accept retail or local office uses.

The ultimate downtown parking solution was created at Post Office Square in Boston, where an obsolete parking garage [139] was replaced by seven levels of underground parking [141], creating a park at street level [140] that has become the centerpiece of the financial district. The city's contribution was not to charge as much money for the garage as it could have obtained by selling it as a development site. The garage and park were financed by a private group, the Friends of Post Office Square, made up mostly of owners of surrounding buildings who wished to guarantee parking spaces

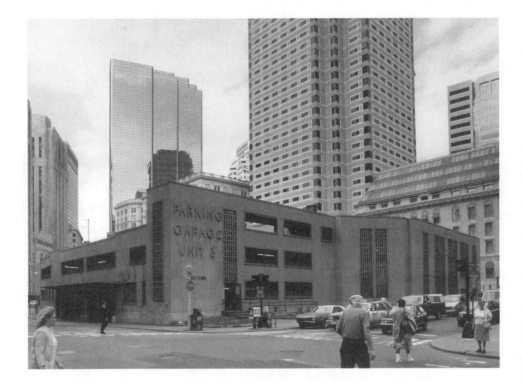

for their tenants and who expected the value of their buildings to rise when the park transformed the area.

If the automobile is an obstacle to creating urbanity in cities, it is even more of a problem in the suburbs, where people are almost completely dependent on cars. A figure-ground drawing of most suburban commercial development shows a great deal more ground than figure. As discussed in chapter 2, it is difficult to develop urbane architectural relationships when three quarters of the land area is devoted to at-grade parking lots. Design guidelines can require build-to lines along a selected street frontage, creating at least one main street with urbane characteristics and relegating parking to side and back streets. Illustration 54 shows how the north portions of the town center at Daniel Island have been planned on this principle.

Suburban residential streets are often dominated by garages and driveways. This problem was identified in the code for Forest Hills

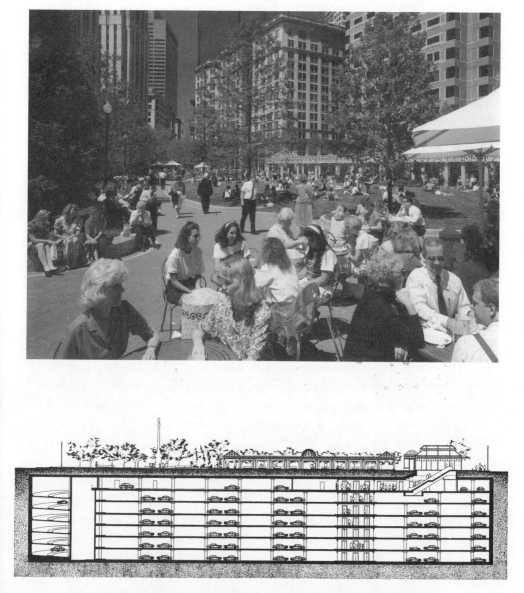

139, 140, 141. In Boston's Post Office Square, an outmoded garage (139) was replaced by a park designed by Halverson Associates (140). Parking is now provided in seven levels underneath the park (141). The Square is now the centerpiece of Boston's financial district; the park and garage were privately financed. The original urban design plan was prepared by Skidmore, Owings & Merrill.

Gardens, the development in the borough of Queens, New York, which exemplified Clarence Perry's neighborhood principles at the beginning of the automobile age. At Forest Hills Gardens, a 60-foot minimum setback for garage doors was required from principal streets and 25 feet from lesser streets. The wisdom of this provision is demonstrated by the unfortunate effect of garages on many modern subdivisions, where the garage doors are placed within a few feet of the right of way. Getting rid of prominent garage doors on small lots may mean using shared driveways for garages at the back of the house, or placing of garages along service lanes or alleys.

The dead-end street is a widely accepted element in suburban land planning. It was made popular in the United States by the plan for Radburn, New Jersey, designed by Clarence Stein and Henry Wright, which grouped the houses around dead-end auto courts and placed the front door of each house along a greenway leading to a park system. Combining cul-de-sacs with a greenway was for a long time considered almost synonymous with good suburban design.

Denouncing the cul-de-sac and the separation of pedestrian ways from streets as absurdities, as Andres Duany does regularly, gets a lot of attention, but sets up an opposition between cul-de-sac and grid, which is actually a misleading discussion.

It was the mindless replication of grid streets in Queens and Brooklyn that caused Clarence Perry to formulate the neighborhood concept. Grids without neighborhoods are not a good large-scale planning system for residential areas. Organizing a site plan into neighborhoods means setting up a special class of arterial streets to define neighborhood districts. These arterials have potential retail locations sited along them, and in other areas run as parkways with a minimum of interruption from driveways and side streets.

An inspection of the plan for Avalon Park in Illustration 51, for example, shows that there is an overall controlling grid of arterial streets, and then a much looser network of subsidiary neighborhood streets, only some of which interconnect from neighborhood to neighborhood. It would be possible to have a Radburn type of plan within the Avalon Park street system; and when you look at the detail of Blount Springs, another Duany, Plater-Zyberk town, there are many cul-de-sacs—a reasonable response to building along ridge lines in a region of steep topography.

The cul-de-sac has some advantages. The four-way intersection is the most dangerous street pattern in a low-density situation; cul-de-sacs produce a safer set of streets for children. The dead-end street pattern also can save the developer money, as the "bulb" at the end of a cul-de-sac gives access to a relatively large number of lots with less paving than access from a conventional street frontage.

However, using the cul-de-sac without the pedestrian greenway produces confusing road systems and makes walking to a house on a different street, or from a house to a school or village center, almost impossible. Unfortunately greenways are now usually omitted, as they have acquired a bad name, being thought of as places where teenagers hang out and play loud music, or, worse, where criminals can ambush the unwary pedestrian or cyclist.

It is to preclude subdivisions that rely on cul-de-sacs without greenways that it becomes necessary to require intersecting streets and sidewalks in neighborhoods. Duany/Plater-Zyberk's design for Belmont in Loudon County, Virginia, shows a connected street and alley plan that is nevertheless hardly a grid [142]. The size of the lot at Belmont determines what type of house can be built, so the subdivision of lots is done on a 16-foot module [143]. In this way different-sized houses can be built within the same guideline system.

The question of safety and public order in greenways is part of the design of a community's public open space plan. The key to safety in public open space is activity, as Jane Jacobs pointed out long ago, a theory that has been validated by many studies since. As long as there are many people about, spaces are overlooked by buildings, and can be seen by passersby, public spaces are safe—unless law and order have broken down completely.

In low-density suburbs, green space does not necessarily have to be public space. Open space plans for Irvington, Illustration 40, and Daniel Island, Illustration 52, demonstrate that reserving environmentally sensitive areas helps create a landscaped setting for devel-

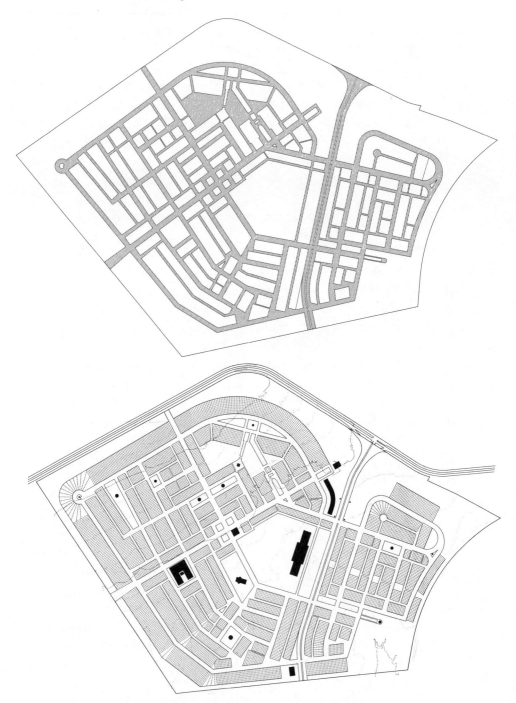

142, 143. Street plan of Belmont, designed by Duany/Plater-Zyberk in Loudon County, Virginia. The building type permitted depends on the size of the lot purchased. Lots are platted in 16-foot modules, so that different building types can co-exist on the same street.

opment, as environmentally sensitive areas are generally part of natural systems that connect to each other. This landscaped setting does not have to be used intensively; in fact, because of environmental sensitivity, use should be controlled by trails or boardwalks.

The street has always been the critical element in the suburban public open space system. Safe streets require close integration with buildings and an environment that is friendly to pedestrians. In suburban areas, many subdivision ordinances require excessive width for streets, as insurance that the streets will continue to be adequate if the residential district should be rebuilt at a higher density. This contingency is very unlikely in most suburbs, and it creates situations where houses are too far from each other to relate well to the street. Subdivision ordinances also tend to require a wide turning radius at the corner so that cars can maintain speed when they make turns and large vehicles like buses or moving vans can stay in one lane as they go around a corner.

Designers find that wide paved areas in streets and a large turning radius are hard to landscape and produce an unpleasant environment for pedestrians, as well as encouraging traffic speeds higher than should take place in residential neighborhoods. Getting planning authorities and traffic engineers to accept lower road speeds, and a local street pattern less suited to large vehicles, permits a return to the street proportions used so successfully in garden suburbs in the days before universal car ownership.

Understanding that streets are part of the public open space network produces designs in which streets lead to parks or important civic locations, or terminate in vistas of the natural landscape. Such designs reinforce public understanding of open spaces and make these spaces more effective.

Similar concerns apply to existing urban street systems, where the automobile and other modern inventions have complicated the design of streets as part of a system of spaces. Eighteenth- and early-nineteenth-century paintings and engravings of city streets show a public space defined by buildings, but this kind of purity of relationship between building and space no longer exists in most cities. Missing from the picture are street lights, traffic signals, street signs, traffic signs, fire hydrants, postal collection boxes, newspaper vending machines, bus-shelters and all the other apparatus of the modern city, not to mention electrical and telephone service wires. These elements are forms of visual noise that can be suppressed from consciousness but are always present in the background of public awareness.

Almost all of the elements that clutter the street are provided by local government, which also owns the street, so in theory there are no obstacles to public control over the design of the streetscape. In practice, each element is controlled by a separate government agency or department, or by a utility company. Design coordination is extremely difficult. Nevertheless, it is possible to set standards for the placement of street lights and other street furniture, for paving, and for the use of landscaping as a mediating factor. The streetscape system should consist of well-designed components organized so they can be implemented consistently. Some of the best examples of a modern streetscape can be found in downtown Portland, Oregon, which has been transformed by policies that redesigned streets. Note the simple but elegant paving, the excellent landscaping, and the unobtrusive system for supporting the trolley wires [144].

How far does the public interest go in regulating the design of individual buildings? Setbacks, build-to lines, requirements for retail continuity are all sufficiently objective that they can be administered as downtown guidelines or even codified in zoning regulations. Standards for location of service entrances and parking can also be set down in zoning, but, since conditions vary from site to site, the actual locations need to be reviewed and approved. It is also possible to require uniform cornice and expression lines on street facades. Experience with the unbroken facades of modern buildings has shown the need for some kind of inflection of long facades, without bringing back the apparatus of the kinds of buildings used by Baron Haussmann in guidelines for Paris. A more abstract system of requirements can make sure that facades are modulated and relate well to public spaces and the street [145, 146].

The kind of suburban codes that relate buildings to lot sizes and street plans, as shown in Illustrations 142 and 143, offer more design

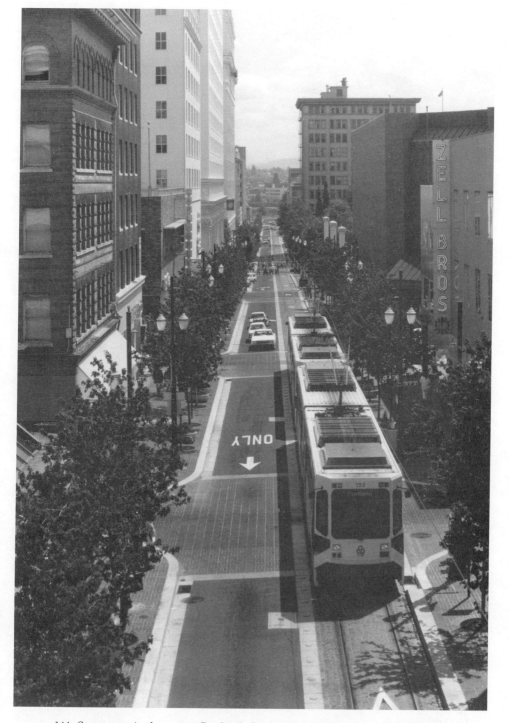

144. *Streetscape in downtown Portland, Oregon, designed by the Zimmer, Gunsul, Frasca Partnership.*

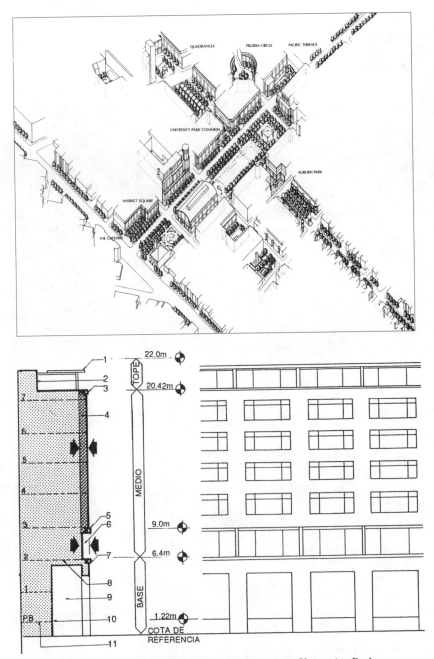

145, 146. *Axonometric drawing showing public spaces at University Park, Cambridge, Massachusetts, planned by Koetter, Kim & Associates and the set of elevation controls by the same firm, in this case for buildings fronting on the boulevard in San Juan described in Illustration 138.*

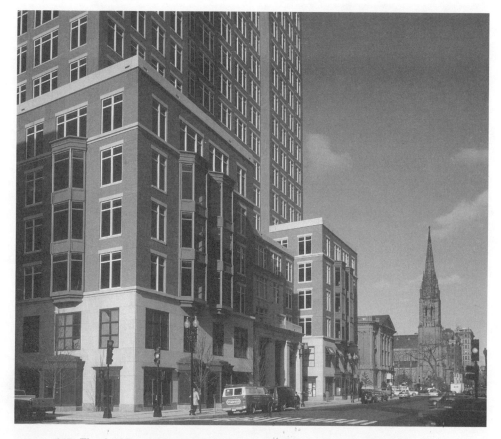

147. This building in Boston by Robert A. M. Stern Architects adopts the strategy of low building masses to define the street and frame the office tower.

guidance than traditional zoning and subdivision. The primary document is the street and lot location plan. Each lot is related to a specific building type, so the placement of lots already says a great deal about the design of the area. More detailed code information is given for each lot type, as well as a set of design standards for each type of street. Again, the relationship of buildings to streets is of primary importance, and these codes also provide section guidelines for different street types that specify relationships such as the distance between the setback/build-to line and the right of way.

Facade-design controls are harder to incorporate into zoning, unless they are part of the control mechanism for a historic district, but can be used in the many situations where property is assembled and sold by a city, or conveyed to a buyer by a private owner as part of a large development.

Facade controls can also be incorporated in guidelines used for review by city art commissions or design review commissions.

In these ways the design of streets, public open spaces, and buildings in both existing cities and new development can be shaped in the public interest.

11

A National Agenda for Action

The politics of federal deficit reduction currently shape the discussion about what can be done for cities and their metropolitan areas. Because little new money can be allocated, policy-makers look to enterprise, or "empowerment," zones, which require no direct public expenditure, to attract business to low-income areas. They are also seeking ways to encourage banks to lend money for development in the inner-city. But there are many other significant policies that require relatively little new funding. There are also ways to make investment in cities and the environment pay for itself in the long run, and, if policies can be seen to pay for themselves, or are evidently necessary for the public welfare, there ought to be a way to finance them.

There is clearly a public interest in the survival of life as we know it on this planet. The argument is between people like Vice President Albert Gore, who contends that the survival of the earth is in the balance right now, and skeptics who say that the planet is a lot more resilient. Ecological analysis describes the environment as in effect a design, established over a long period of time through the complex interactions of many different factors. Changing one element can change all the others. Extending a runway from Kennedy Airport into Jamaica Bay disturbs an important stopping point on the flyways of various species of birds, with incalculable consequences to the habitat at both ends of the migratory pattern. Gore's book begins with the image of ships lying in the desert between Kazakhstan and Uzbekistan in the former Soviet Union, where badly planned irrigation policies have left fishing boats stranded on the sandy bottom of what was until recently the Aral Sea. If the consequences of destabilizing natural systems are unknown, and possibly disastrous, it makes sense to conserve the existing equilibrium as much as possible. Conservatism, literally, would seem to be the appropriate public policy.

This assumption leads to policies that conserve watersheds, forests, and agricultural land, plus regulations requiring approved plans and permits for extensive regrading or tree cutting, restrictions on development of steep slopes or soils subject to erosion, and requirements for control and treatment of water runoff.

The urban growth boundary is the essential first step both to conserve the environment and to turn development attention back toward areas that are already urbanized or partly urbanized. It is possible to make arguments for growth boundaries and other elements of state planning based solely on efficient use of public funds, but growth boundaries are also a way of insuring survival of the natural environment. That is a significant additional public purpose. A growth boundary can be adopted through negotiation among the different communities in a metropolitan area, but it is much more likely to happen if mandated by state planning legislation.

The adoption of state planning laws in all 50 states is thus a precondition for urban growth boundaries as a national planning policy. Regional compacts to cover metropolitan areas that include parts of several states will also be necessary. The states that have already adopted planning legislation include many of the areas that have needed it the most, heavily populated states on either the East or West Coast. Many of these states are conservative politically; but people have understood the necessity of bringing urban growth under some kind of control.

The federal Coastal Zone Management Act of 1972 is a model for possible federal legislation encouraging the creation of state plans. Currently 29 of the 34 states with coastlines have adopted management policies that meet the standards of the Act. The legislation does not mandate that states comply, and the incentives are relatively inexpensive: chiefly federal funds for preparing and administering the plan. Federal grants for the preparation of state plans that include growth boundaries would be a relatively inexpensive way of promoting a major change in national priorities.

While growth boundaries for metropolitan areas are essential, too restricted a boundary for the city at the center can be a serious problem. David Rusk, in his book, *Cities Without Suburbs*, presents statistics from 320 metropolitan areas to demonstrate that cities whose suburbs are mainly beyond the city limits have far more severe economic and social problems than cities that have been able to annex their suburbs or whose boundaries are so loosely drawn that most suburban development is still within the city. City governments that include most of the metropolitan area have greater financial resources because much of the new city is still within the same boundaries as the old city. Another important factor: elected officials represent their constituents. The government of a suburban community will represent only the immediate interests of the suburb; a metropolitan government—like the one that resulted when Indianapolis merged with Marion County—will represent the interests of the region.

Regional revenue sharing based on state-mandated revenue equalization formulas represent an alternative to metropolitan consolidation. The prototype is Minnesota's 1971 law covering 188 municipalities in the seven-county Minneapolis–St. Paul area. Forty percent of the annual increase in taxes on commercial and industrial property above the 1971 assessment base is paid into a fund that is redistributed among the 188 communities according to a formula based on population and relative property values. States have the power to pass such laws for any metropolitan area. If the inequalities of funding for school districts, for example, can be smoothed out in this way, schools in poorer districts have an opportunity to improve, reducing a major cause of migration from the old city to the new.

Restoring natural ecosystems in urbanized areas is both an environmental and a social policy. Turning large areas of derelict industrial land into park can not only improve air and water quality, but also create value in surrounding properties, which, in turn, can encourage banks to lend to projects in the area. The construction costs for the Mystic River Reservation described in chapter 7 were $62,500 an acre. If land values in urban neighborhoods are relatively low, there is a good possibility of using some version of tax-increment financing to promote environmental restoration in urban areas. As the Mystic River project clearly demonstrates, re-creating natural river edges or parkland can transform the setting for adjacent neighborhoods. In principle, environmental restoration is economically feasible if its costs can be amortized by taxes on the increased property values created, although there needs to be a mechanism for overcoming the risk that an immediate property tax increase could stop the very redevelopment needed to pay for the investment. Similar principles apply to the need for public assistance in cleaning up toxic wastes, a major obstacle to redeveloping disused urban industrial land. Government funds for environmental cleanup should be keyed to the economic potential of the redeveloped land. It should be possible to pay for such programs from the increased property values created.

Environmental restoration is also important in suburban and rural areas, where there are often toxic residues from mining and manufacturing operations. Redesign of derelict land can transform suburban neighborhoods, as shown by a park in Liberty, Illinois, designed by Marian Weiss and Michael Manfredi [148, 149]. A small recreation area and a fragment of farm land partly used as a nursery garden becomes the centerpiece for a whole area.

Because so much of the future of cities and towns is directed by private real estate investment, development regulation is a primary element in any agenda for change. While development regulation is a jealously guarded local prerogative, state planning agencies can require local governments to revise their codes in accordance with standards set by the state, while the local government retains autonomy in administering the code. State plans should call for local governments to build environmental protection into their development ordinances by revising zoning and subdivision regulations to treat land as an eco-system, and not just a commodity. Local subdivision ordinances also need revision, to keep the standards for street grades from requiring the bulldozing of whole properties. Awareness of regional environmental planning considerations creates a public purpose for regulations that encourage compact neighborhoods with a mix of housing types, and dense, mixed-use commercial centers. Such compact communities also support rapid transit, a further justification for enlarging the purpose of zoning and subdivision from a mediating role to an affirmative one, incorporating models like the Traditional Neighborhood Development ordinance described in chapter 4.

Writing these ordinances is so tedious that most jurisdictions follow a few basic model codes, adapting them as required to fit local circumstances. There thus needs to be a new model environmental zoning ordinance of the type described in chapter 3, plus a model grading ordinance and tree preservation ordinance to prevent developers from making an end-run around the environmental preservation requirements before they seek development approval, and new model community design codes.

The American Law Institute completed work on a model land development code in 1975. It has been influential in encouraging state planning legislation; but its proposals for local laws mostly concerned fairness and uniform administration, not specific zoning and subdivision provisions. What is required now is a much more detailed set of prototypes for local ordinances; their creation should involve not only lawyers, but designers and environmentalists. The need for improving the fundamental structure and procedures of zoning and other development regulations is made more urgent by the Supreme Court's 1994 decision in *Dolan v. Tigard* that sets a stricter standard of judicial scrutiny for local land use decisions.

States should also pass enabling legislation to permit drawing up specific plans, like the California specific plan legislation described in chapter 5.

State planning legislation, model environmental zoning ordinances, affirmative models for zoning and subdivision, plus specific plan legislation for existing areas, are not expensive in comparison with the costs of most government programs. The costs for private investors are also not large. Environmental and design-based changes in regulations may well make private investments more productive by concentrating development in the most suitable locations. While there will be some changes in land values and procedures, the real estate market has adjusted to much bigger changes in the past.

Transportation, the next item on our agenda, does require the commitment of substantial government money; the questions are: How much is needed? How can available funds be used as effectively as possible?

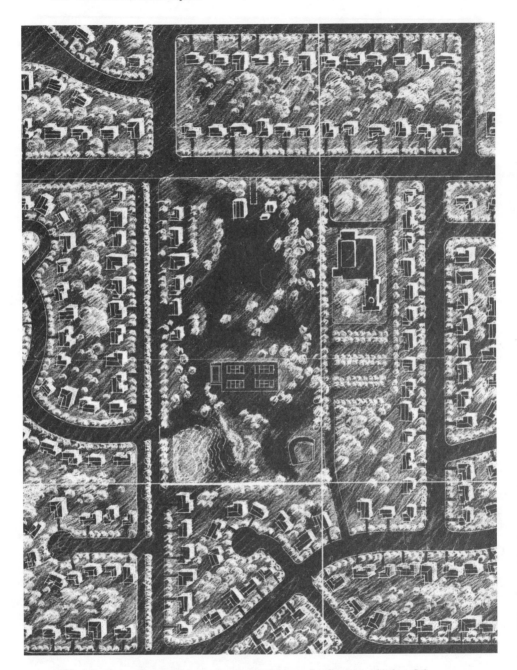

148, 149. *A small recreation area and a fragment of a farm in suburban Liberty,*
Illinois, becomes a community park that gives focus to an entire neighborhood.
The designers are Marian Weiss and Michael Manfredi.

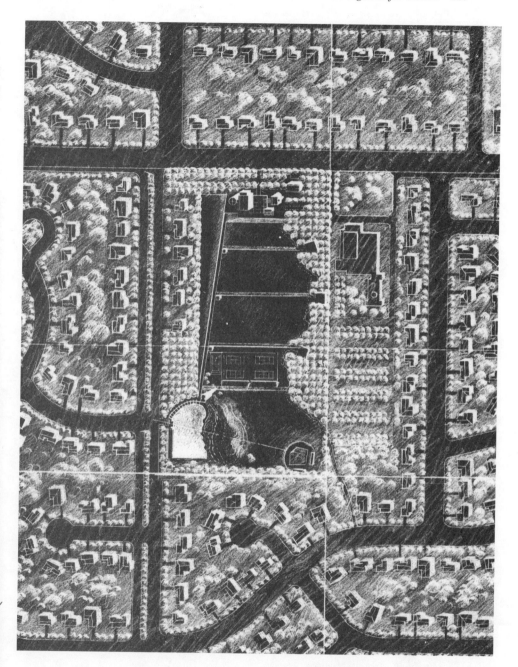

When local rapid transit ceased to be profitable, the public sector took it over. Now, much public transportation is operated like a charity, providing the minimum necessary in circumstances that are often inconvenient and humiliating, but considered good enough for people who have no alternative. Despite the importance of providing affordable transportation to match people to jobs in an ever-expanding metropolitan area, it has been hard to fund transportation as a social policy. However, 55 people sitting on a bus use a lot less fuel and cause much less pollution than the same number of people in private cars; a two-car trolley uses even less fuel per passenger; an eight-car train is yet more efficient in improving air quality and conserving fossil fuels. People do choose public transit over private cars when the alternative is more attractive: the private express buses that take Manhattanites to resort towns on Long Island, the Washington Metro, the BART system. What these exceptions demonstrate is that passenger comfort, speed, frequency of service, a reasonable price, and proximity of stops to destinations are all required.

Most of the new employment centers, the accidental cities created in formerly suburban areas over the last generation, can only be reached by automobile. They are a long and difficult commute from many older urban neighborhoods; and communication between these new centers and established downtowns is also difficult. Many of the new centers are also becoming too big to be served by the automobile alone, as demonstrated by perpetual suburban traffic congestion. Without transit systems to alleviate gridlock and link the old and the new city, the fragmentation of the metropolitan area is likely to become worse: with fewer jobs and a declining tax base in the old city, increasing demands for road construction in the new, and businesses moving on to what they hope will be less congested areas. Money spent on a mass transit system now is thus likely to save other expenditures later: for road construction and relocation in the new city, and preservation of the economy and social services of the older urban areas.

Other countries, like Japan and France, recognize that regional transportation is a major economic development tool. The planning strategy for the Île-de-France, the metropolitan area around Paris, relies on public transportation systems to tie together housing and

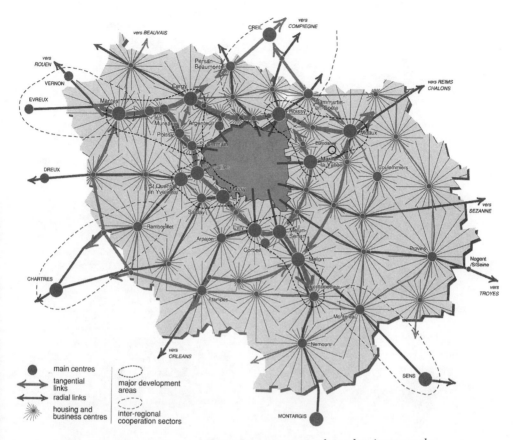

150. A map showing how transportation systems are planned to integrate the Paris metropolitan area.

business centers, major development areas, and what the plan calls inter-regional cooperation areas [150].

The federal Intermodal Surface Transportation Efficiency Act of 1991 (ISTEA) gives local governments in the U.S. their first committed source of funds that can be used not just for highways but for a variety of transit or traffic improvements. Communities now have the ability to design and implement a transportation system that meets local needs and conditions. This brilliant piece of legislation has been needed for a long time, but the procedures it opens up are so unfamiliar to administrators that few localities have yet begun to make good use of them. Another difficulty is that the $31.5 billion committed over six years is not enough to create integrated

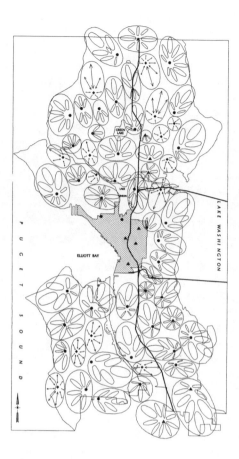

151. *The proposed neighborhood circulation concept in the Seattle Comprehensive Plan.*

transportation systems for every metropolitan area in the country. No one knows how much covering the whole country would cost; the only way to find out is for each metropolitan area to emulate the process gone through in the Seattle metropolitan region, described in chapter 3, a process that is as much about growth boundaries and land planning as it is about transportation. The city of Seattle itself is preparing a new comprehensive plan that is based on dividing the city into neighborhood districts, called urban villages in the plan, linking every urban village to every other, to the city center, and to the new regional transit systems [151].

The easiest way to create an effective public transportation system in the new city is likely to be with bus routes. The bus can make local stops in a residential neighborhood, run express to a destination, and then make several stops in the new city where the development is far more diffuse than in a traditional downtown. The identification of the most important destinations is a critical step, one that in turn will do much to set future development patterns.

When a second generation of development has taken place in the new city, according to plans and ordinances which promote compact and concentrated development in selected locations, it may be possible to create a new rail network. In the meantime, the plebeian bus, rather than the glamorous train or the nostalgia-inducing trolley, probably provides the best value for money. A community can buy a fleet of approximately 100 buses for the cost of a mile of surface rail track or 500 buses for a mile of subsurface rapid transit—and that is just one mile of track, without the trains. The Washington Metro, which is a true regional system, will have just over 100 miles of track when it is completed, and has taken an entire generation to build. Ultimately every metropolitan region in the U.S. should have the equivalent of the Washington Metro; in the meantime, buses are an undervalued alternative to rail rapid transit. It is true that buses have a bad reputation, but frequent service, express routes, and good maintenance can overcome negative preconceptions, as demonstrated by systems in such cities as Pittsburgh, New Orleans, Denver, and Seattle.

Where the tracks already exist, the economics may swing in favor of rail-rapid transit; but the population along the tracks has to be dense enough, or be planned for densities great enough, to support a rapid transit system, population densities of at least 10 families to the acre within easy walking or driving distance of each station. Adding environmental conservation and the reduction of air pollution to social equity considerations makes a stronger argument for rail transit, leading, for example, to the multi-billion dollar investment for a new rail transit system in Los Angeles.

Assuming that the interstate highway system, the national air transport system, and national passenger rail service continue to be funded and to be improved, the other federal transportation initiative that could make a major difference for older cities would be improvements in rail freight routes. Greater international trade has meant an enormous increase in container shipments coming into port cities and shipped to long-distance destinations by rail. The latest rail technology double-stacks containers on freight cars.

Many older urban rail corridors do not have the height and width clearances necessary to accommodate double-stack freight trains. Lack of access for these trains negates one of the great advantages of bypassed urban industrial areas, their proximity to railway tracks. While enterprise zones that provide relief from some taxation and some bureaucratic restrictions can be used to encourage job-creation in older urban areas, it is also important for industry to have the appropriate supporting infrastructure, and urban sites often have difficult access patterns for trucks.

Capital funds for infrastructure repair are also a continual necessity for the old city, and new infrastructure investment is required to support existing growth in the new city. In the next few years many urban highway viaducts and interchanges will be nearing the end of their useful life. They will either require expensive repairs, or permit an opportunity for reconsidering some of the dubious planning decisions that produced them in the first place.

Net investment in infrastructure of all kinds in the United States, including transportation, currently is less than 2 percent of GNP, as opposed to 5.7 percent in Japan and 3.7 percent in Germany. Of course, Germany and Japan do not have the military responsibilities of the United States, but the comparisons are instructive. In designing a national program for infrastructure support it is important for localities to identify what they need; no one at present has an accurate picture of how much money the United States should be investing in urban infrastructure, or what the most immediate priorities ought to be.

Urban neighborhoods with a high concentration of crime, deteriorated housing, and other serious problems remain the most critical obstacle to putting metropolitan areas back together.

Since the Great Depression of the 1930s there has been a public consensus in the United States that no one should be allowed to go hungry or without shelter. And, until recently, that promise seemed to have been kept. The large numbers of homeless people to be seen today in almost every city show that something has gone wrong with the social safety net. Homelessness seems to be part of the general breakdown of community in the old city, the result of the interaction of changes in mental-health care, a shortage of cheap hotels, drugs, unemployment, and a lack of effective social services.

Public policies that relied solely on physical improvement of housing conditions have proved to be naive, but deteriorated housing continues to be a serious problem. Housing conditions that do not meet the building code are illegal. The danger of a strictly legal approach is that it can encourage demolition rather than repair; but public policy should not permit obvious violations of the law to persist for years. The problem of illegal housing conditions is particularly urgent when the public is subsidizing them through welfare payments to tenants in substandard buildings; it is even more urgent when the public owns the building, as is the case in many deteriorated housing projects. As discussed in chapter 8, the long-term solution is to correct the original mistakes in design and management that make the buildings so difficult to maintain. Ultimately ways must be found to finance the conversion of all housing projects into neighborhoods and communities, while keeping their role as a supply of affordable housing.

A big public investment in renovating government-owned housing is essential over the next generation. The fractured metropolis cannot be put together without it.

What prevents renovated housing from deteriorating again? Part of the issue is management, and the creation of a community among the residents. Some low-income people should be helped to move out of areas where poverty is concentrated, leaving room for all inner-city neighborhoods to become mixed-income communities. There needs to be sufficient national support for social welfare policies that cities are not forced into diverting revenues to welfare that should be used for annual maintenance of public housing, as well as streets, infrastructure, parks, government buildings, and schools.

But many urban neighborhoods deteriorated because of the blighting influence of industry, railway, and highway viaducts, or electrical power lines and substations. These conditions need to be corrected, as described in chapter 8, as part of the renovation of these neighborhoods. Investments in landscaping and other buffers that limit adverse impacts of industry, highways, railroads, and power lines have a public purpose in overcoming incentives to disinvestment and raising adjacent property values. Using natural systems to enhance air and water quality in already-urbanized areas requires environmental restoration; a new idea, but there is clearly a public purpose in such investment if it promotes public health. Without such measures, other investments in restoring the old city will be in jeopardy.

The failure of schools in inner-city areas perpetuates their tragedies. Establishing national educational standards, and overcoming entrenched funding inequalities, will help give everyone equal access to a good education. The Headstart program is one Great Society measure that clearly has worked, although it has never been funded to cover all the children who need it, and some children seem to lose the benefits of their head start when they get to later grades in underfunded, poorly run schools. What is needed is more money for Headstart. As discussed in chapter 8, many of the other problems of inner-city education also come down to lack of funding. Inner-city schools need more, not less, money than suburban school districts, because these schools need to provide security guards, meals, after-school programs, and other support services, as well as the equipment and textbooks that are too often unavailable. As the example of the Harriet Tubman school described in chapter 8 demonstrates, the additional funding increments may not be that large, but they are essential. In addition to regional revenue-sharing systems for school districts, there need to be national programs to supplement budgets for schools in areas that can't achieve the necessary standards on their own.

Because the school system is such an important factor in determining residential locations, which in turn drive location decisions by business and industry, investments in a local school system are economic development decisions. It may make sense for a community to put more money into its schools rather than to offer subsidies to factories.

The entrepreneurial policies cities have been using to keep downtowns operating also make a good model for suburban communities and small towns that are under pressure from shopping centers, and

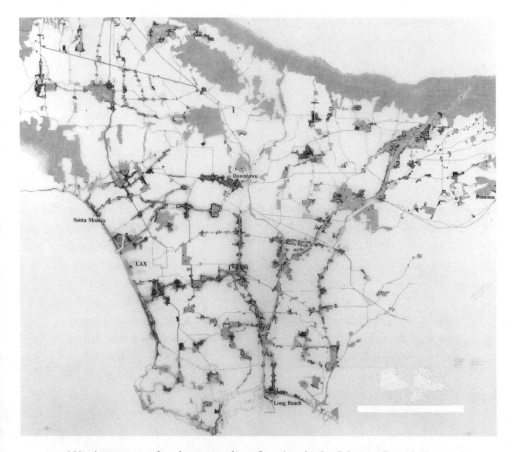

152. *A greenway plan for metropolitan Los Angeles by Johnson, Fain & Pereira Associates.*

need to develop techniques to make their central areas competitive again. Continuing support of the arts has proved vital to sustaining older urban centers, and will come to be equally important for new centers as they mature. For all centers, design guidelines like those described in chapter 10 are needed to fit old and new development together into a coherent pattern. Standards for street lights, traffic signals, and landscaping are also essential to the design of every city and town. These expenditures are made in any case; they might as well be done right. The definition of the public interest already includes economic development, and the experience of cities in managing downtowns to enhance their competitive position has established that investment in attractions and design guidelines are important to keeping downtowns competitive in a time when many business-location decisions have become discretionary. As in education, there can be national standards for environmental and urban planning and design that cities can meet to become eligible for supplemental funding.

The environmental movement could be a strong political constituency for the maintenance and restoration of the old city. As people become more concerned about managing the environment so that it can sustain future generations, there should be increasing concern not only for matching development intensity to the carrying capacity of the land, but for making the best possible use of existing urban development—not only to divert growth away from further invasion of the natural landscape, but to avoid duplicating existing streets and services in a new location. Environmental conservatism leads to a policy of preserving old buildings, not just because they may be of historic or architectural interest, but because they represent a commitment of natural resources. Old buildings have value: they were bought and paid for long ago; their stone, steel, wood, and copper are hard to salvage and would need to be replaced, the debris from demolition overloads scarce landfill locations. The appropriate new regulatory policy would be to require findings of necessity before a demolition permit could be issued, as is done now for structures designated as landmarks or buildings in a historic district. It is also time to change tax policies that too often make a parking lot on the site of a demolished building more profitable than keeping the building in operation.

The same kinds of environmental arguments can be made for restoring old neighborhoods and making better use of bypassed areas as can be made for conserving old buildings. Adding environmental conservatism to already powerful social-equity arguments enlarges the constituency for making new investments in inner-city education, housing, and amenities. Unless urban problems in the old city are brought under control, growth pressures on the natural environment at the metropolitan fringe are not going to let up.

Improving the new city and restoring the old deal with two parts of the same problem and need to go forward simultaneously. The sooner these issues are faced, the less costly their solution will be in both money and social conflict.

Suggestions for Additional Reading

The literature of city and regional planning is extensive, as are writings about the history, theory and practice of architecture and landscape architecture. Such related subjects as political science, sociology, environmental psychology, urban geography or real-estate economics have their own specialized literature. Anything like a complete bibliography for any one of these specialties would be overwhelming; keeping up with all of them is a full-time job. The following is a short list of readily available, readable books that are introductions to various aspects of city design and development. They will, in turn, refer the reader to many other possible sources.

Alexander, Christopher: *The Timeless Way of Building*, Oxford University Press, 1979; and (with five associated authors) *A Pattern Language*, Oxford University Press, 1977. Alexander and his associates believe that there are basic principles that can be derived from the best architecture and settlements created in the past. These principles form a syntax for "patterns" that can be used as the words in a language of design and construction. You are meant to read *The Timeless Way* first, although it was published after *A Pattern Language*. These books are part of an extraordinarily ambitious effort by Alexander and his associates to define a theory of architecture, and of landscape and city design. There are many valuable insights in these books, but they can be infuriating because they make ex-cathedra pronouncements on complicated issues. There is also a strong bias against modern, industrialized society.

Arendt, Randall with Elizabeth Brabec, Harry L. Dodson, Christine Reid, and Robert D. Yaro: *Rural by Design: Maintaining Small Town Character*, American Planning Association, 1994. This work is an outgrowth of an earlier study of managing change in the Connecticut River valley. The authors demonstrate that rural character can be maintained, or an area can be urbanized, depending on how new development is designed and placed.

Calthorpe, Peter: *The Next American Metropolis*, Princeton Architectural Press, 1993. A very useful compilation of urban and regional design solutions devised by Calthorpe and his associates in their professional practice. They demonstrate clearly the advantages of walkable, mixed-use communities connected to each other by rapid transit as well as by streets and highways.

Duany, Andres and Elizabeth Plater-Zyberk: *Towns and Town-Making Principles*, a catalogue distributed by Rizzoli of an exhibition at the Harvard Graduate School of Design in 1991. This volume is just a place-holder for a more comprehensive manifesto that will doubtless be pub-lished in the future. In the meantime, those with good eyesight and a magnifying lens can puzzle out the design principles and implementation codes for thirteen communities planned by the authors.

Garreau, Joel: *Edge City*, Doubleday, 1991. An outstanding piece of reporting about what has been happening to American suburbs and metro-politan regions. Using interviews, observation and inference, Garreau gives a much clearer description than can be found in works by profes-sional social scientists who feel obligated to organize information accord-ing to abstract mathematical or statistical models. Garreau is a sophis-ticated observer as well as a good story-teller: one of the high points of the book is his interview with Christopher Alexander.

Gore, Al: *Earth in the Balance: Ecology and the Human Spirit*, Hough-ton, Mifflin, 1992. This is a serious, well-balanced introduction to the policies that might correct major environmental problems such as climate changes created by industrial pollution, depletion of the ozone layer, and threats to the world's food supplies. It is not a collection of speeches or position papers. A U.S. Senator, as Gore was when he wrote the book, is in a good position to get hold of the latest research and to talk to experts around the world.

Hall, Peter G.: *Urban and Regional Planning*, Wiley, 1975. This text is now out of date, but it remains an elegantly concise introduction to the virtues and limitations of planning techniques used in England and France after World War II, and the relation of these techniques to planning practice in the U.S. Hall is the author of other excellent books, including *Great Planning Disasters*, Weidenfeld and Nicholson, 1980.

Hiss, Tony: *The Experience of Place*, Knopf, 1990. A charmingly written personal account of the author's own experience of places, his research into the history of representative special places, and his interviews with people who are trying to preserve buildings and landscapes, and to im-prove new development.

Jackson, J. B., *A Sense of Place, A Sense of Time*, Yale University Press, 1994. The latest collection of essays by an acute and original observer of life in the U.S. Basically, anything by J. B. Jackson is well worth reading.

Jacobs, Jane: *The Death and Life of Great American Cities*, Vintage Books, first published in 1961. Many seemingly axiomatic observations about cities, such as the need to stop destroying neighborhoods to build express highways and the importance of encouraging mixed-use districts and lively streets, were first given articulate expression in this book. However, you should also read "Home Remedies for Urban Cancer," by the urban historian and critic Lewis Mumford, a review that first appeared in *The New Yorker* for December 1, 1961, and is reprinted in Mumford's *The Urban Prospect*, Harcourt, Brace, 1968.

Katz, Peter: *The New Urbanism*, McGraw-Hill, 1994. A beautifully illustrated compendium of work by Peter Calthorpe, Duany/Plater-Zyberk and other designers with a succinct introductory history by Todd Bressi and an afterword by Vincent Scully. The only problem with this book is that it presents exceptional work as if there were no reason why it should not become the norm. It glosses over the problems that will prevent many of the projects illustrated from being built as shown, or ever being built at all. Scully's afterword strikes a proper note of skepticism.

Kelbaugh, Douglas, ed.: *The Pedestrian Pocket Book*, Princeton Architectural Press, 1989. This book provides versions by several different designers of some of the concepts elaborated by Peter Calthorpe in *The Next American Metropolis*.

Kostof, Spiro: *The City Shaped* and *The City Assembled*, Bulfinch Press, Little, Brown, 1991, 1992. These two extraordinarily well illustrated source books of city design concepts are a monumental work of scholarship. Kostof felt that if city designers are going to draw inspiration from historical examples, they should be reliably informed about them.

Kunstler, James: *The Geography of Nowhere*, Simon and Schuster, 1993. Anyone who thinks that current real-estate and planning practice are basically sound should read this scathing critique.

Lang, Jon: *Urban Design: The American Experience*, Van Nostrand Reinhold, 1994. An attempt to put a discussion of every issue related to urban design in the U.S. into a single volume. Impossible, of course, but the encyclopedic intention makes this a useful reference book.

Langdon, Philip: *A Better Place to Live: Reshaping the American Suburb*, University of Massachusetts Press, 1994. A well-written analysis of what is wrong with current suburban development, and of the methods and designs needed to improve it.

Lynch, Kevin: *A Theory of Good City Form*, MIT Press, 1981. How do you decide whether one city design is better than another? What is a good city? Lynch attempts to define the terms of the discussion as well as the means of determining the answers. While these philosophical issues can never be settled definitively, they are of central importance to every decision made about the future of cities and regions. Lynch was also the author of other significant books, including *Site Planning*, currently available in its third edition, co-written with Gary Hack and published by MIT Press, 1983.

Rusk, David: *Cities Without Suburbs*, Woodrow Wilson Center Press, 1993. Rusk, the former mayor of Albuquerque, presents a convincing statistical analysis to demonstrate that (to use the terminology I have used in my own book) cities that are large enough to incorporate the new cities that have grown up in their suburbs, or are part of some kind of metropolitan government, are more successful in dealing with problems of poverty and crime than an old city that is confined to outmoded boundaries and separated from the new city. "Inner cities should not have to assume the role of sole providers for the poor. That must become the responsibility of the whole metro area—city and suburbs, cities without suburbs."

Scully, Vincent: *Architecture: The Natural and the Manmade*, St. Martin's, 1991. An eloquent introduction to some of the great historical issues of architecture and of landscape and city design. Scully is also the author of many other important studies in architectural history; this book is in some ways a summary of ideas he has developed in more detail elsewhere.

Solomon, Daniel: *ReBuilding*, Princeton Architectural Press, 1992. The author is an architect who specializes in urban design and housing, and the plans for his buildings are well worth study. But what is really exceptional about this book is the text: funny, sincere and right on target.

Sorkin, Michael: *Local Code*, Princeton Architectural Press, 1993. Sorkin, known for his incisive critical essays about architecture, has decided to describe a utopian city by means of a set of development regulations. Both the vision and the code are highly idiosyncratic, but provide a good demonstration that building and zoning codes embody important theoretical issues; they are not just boring housekeeping tasks. Sorkin is also the editor of *Variations on a Theme Park*, Hill and Wang, 1992, which turns a skeptical eye on the way artfully designed environments in commercial developments are not substitutes for authentic places or the traditional public realm.

Spirn, Anne Whiston, *The Granite Garden: Urban Nature and Human Design*, Basic Books/Harper Colophon Books, 1984. Cities are also natural environments, Anne Spirn reminds us in this gracefully written text full of sensible advice about improving urban air and water quality, relating development to the carrying capacity of the environment, nurturing parks and trees and integrating cities into the regional ecosystem.

Stern, Robert A. M. with John Montague Massengale: "The Anglo-American Suburb," in *Architectural Design*, October–November 1981. Stern has been an important influence in reminding city designers what successful places some early 20th-century suburbs have turned out to be. This special issue of an architectural magazine is a handy assemblage of views and plans.

Whyte, William H.: *City*, Doubleday, 1988. Whyte has been a pioneer in looking at how people actually inhabit and use urban spaces and then suggesting design improvements based on his observations.

Zukin, Sharon: *Landscapes of Power*, University of California Press, 1991. This socio-political critique of post-industrial development in the U.S. administers a useful intellectual jolt to anyone who thinks "the new urbanism" is a completely benign process.

Illustration Credits

1, 2: Drawings made under direction of Jonathan Barnett by Michael Faulhaber, Florida Center for Community Development
3: Photo courtesy Friendswood Development Corporation
4–9: Drawings copyright © Regional Plan Association/Dodson Associates, used by permission of Regional Plan Association
10, 11: Drawings courtesy University of South Florida
12: Drawing © Duany/Plater-Zyberk, used by permission
13, 14: Drawings courtesy University of South Florida
15: Photo by Maxwell MacKenzie, courtesy RTKL
16: Drawing courtesy RTKL
17, 18: Photos courtesy Cooper, Carry & Associates
19: Drawing courtesy Cooper, Carry & Associates
20, 21: Drawings courtesy Bernard Tschumi
22, 23: Drawings by Randy Hollingsworth, courtesy Hanson and Taylor
24: Drawing © Duany/Plater-Zyberk, used by permission
25, 26: Drawings courtesy Johnson, Fain & Pereira Associates
27, 28: Drawings courtesy University of South Florida
29, 30: Drawings courtesy UDA Architects
31, 32: Photos courtesy UDA Architects
33: Drawing courtesy UDA Architects
34, 35: Drawings courtesy Center for Rural Massachusetts
36–40: Drawings courtesy Jonathan Barnett and Steven Kent Peterson
41: Map courtesy Greenbelt Alliance
42–44: Drawings courtesy Puget Sound Council of Governments
45: Drawing courtesy GBQC Architects
46: Drawing courtesy Duany/Plater-Zyberk
47: Drawing from the New York Regional Survey and Plan of 1929, used by permission
48, 49: Drawings courtesy Calthorpe Associates
50: Photo courtesy Duany/Plater-Zyberk
51: Drawing courtesy Duany/Plater-Zyberk
52–54: Drawings courtesy Cooper, Robertson + Partners
55–57: Drawings courtesy ROMA Design Group
58: Drawing courtesy Sedway Cooke Associates
59, 60: Drawings courtesy Zimmer, Gunsul, Frasca Partnership

61–67: Drawings made under direction of Jonathan Barnett by Derold Polston

68–72: Drawings made by students at University of Maryland for research seminar directed by Jonathan Barnett

73, 74: Drawings made under direction of Jonathan Barnett by Derold Polston

75: Photo courtesy Gruen Associates

76, 77: Drawings from *Centers for the Urban Environment* by Victor Gruen, used by permission of Van Nostrand Reinhold

78: Drawing courtesy ELS Design Group

79: Photo by Scott McDonald, Hedrich Blessing, courtesy of RTKL Associates

80–82: Drawings courtesy RTKL Associates

83–85: Drawings courtesy City of Norfolk

86: M.D. Arnold photo courtesy Norfolk Redevelopment and Housing Authority

87: Photo courtesy McCormick Barron

88: Drawing courtesy ROMA Design Group

89, 90: Photos courtesy ROMA Design Group

91: Drawing courtesy Chan, Krieger Associates

92, 93: Photos by the Hursley Office

94: Photo by Swain Edens, courtesy of Hartman-Cox

95: Drawing courtesy SOM

96: Drawing courtesy Robert A. M. Stern Architects

97, 98: Photos courtesy UDA Architects

99: Photo by John Gustavson, courtesy Carol R. Johnson and Associates

100: Map courtesy Carol R. Johnson and Associates

101, 102: Drawings courtesy Lane, Frenchman Associates

103: Photo by Felice Frankel

104: Drawing courtesy Hanna, Olin

105: Photo courtesy SOM

106: Drawing courtesy SOM

107: Photo by Geonex Cartwright Aerial Surveys

108: Drawing courtesy ROMA Design Group

109: Photo by Alex S. Maclean, Landslides, used by permission

110: Drawing courtesy Boston Redevelopment Authority

111: Photo © Steve Rosenthal, used by permission

112: Photo by Anton Grassi, courtesy Goody, Clancy & Associates

113, 114: Drawings courtesy Goody, Clancy & Associates

115, 116: Drawings courtesy UDA Architects

117: Photo courtesy UDA Architects

118: Photo by Tom Reiss, courtesy Liebman/Melting Partnership

119: Drawing courtesy Liebman/Melting Partnership

120, 121: Drawings courtesy Rob Wellington Quigley

122, 123: Photos courtesy Stull and Lee

124: Photo by Andrew Squire, Landslides, used by permission
125: Photo © Steve Rosenthal, used by permission
126: Drawing from *Paris project* no. 13–14 as reproduced by Norma Evenson in *Paris: A Century of Change, 1878–1978,* published by the Yale University Press.
127: Photo by Jerry Spearman, collection of the author
128: Drawing courtesy Cleveland City Planning Commission
129: Drawing courtesy Cesar Pelli & Associates
130: Photo © Peter Aaron/ESTO, used by permission
131: Drawing courtesy Koetter, Kim & Associates
132: Photo © Ed Stoecklein, used by permission
133: Drawing courtesy Cesar Pelli & Associates
134: Drawing courtesy Cleveland City Planning Commission
135, 136: Drawings courtesy HNTB
137, 138: Drawings courtesy Koetter, Kim & Associates
139: Photo by Bill Horsman, courtesy Friends of Post Office Square
140: Photo by Peter Vanderwarker, courtesy Friends of Post Office Square
141: Drawing courtesy Halverson Associates
142, 143: Drawings courtesy Duany/Plater-Zyberk
144: Photo courtesy Zimmer, Gunsul, Frasca Partnership
145, 146: Drawings courtesy Koetter, Kim & Associates
147: Photo © Peter Aaron/ESTO, used by permission
148, 149: Drawings courtesy Weiss, Manfredi Architects
150: Map courtesy French Government Information Services
151: Drawing courtesy Seattle Planning Department
152: Photo by Brian Forrest of a drawing by Johnson, Fain & Pereira Associates, courtesy Johnson, Fain & Pereira Associates

Index